# SHARPEN UP YOUR INTERVIEWING

# SHARPEN UP YOUR INTERVIEWING
## The systematic approach to effective interviewing for busy managers

### JACK GRATUS

MERCURY

First published in 1991
by Mercury Books
Gold Arrow Publications Limited,
862 Garratt Lane, London SW17 0NB

Set in Sabon by Phoenix Photosetting
Printed and bound in Great Britain by
Mackays of Chatham PLC, Chatham, Kent

*British Library Cataloguing in Publication Data*

Gratus, Jack
    Sharpen up your interviewing.
    1. Personnel. Interviewing
    I. Title
    658.31124

ISBN 1–85251–024–2

# CONTENTS

# INTRODUCTION: AN INTERVIEW WITH THE READER

As this is a book about interviewing, it is appropriate to start with a short interview.

**What kind of interviews do you conduct?**
Say 'interviewing' to most managers and they tend to think of recruiting. In fact, in the course of the day you may conduct a wide variety of interviews. You may start interviewing for a new assistant; over lunch you could be interviewing a potential client for new business; the afternoon may be spent solving a staff problem in which interviewing (without you realising it) plays a crucial role; and the day could end with an appraisal interview of an employee to determine his or her future in the company.

One way or another, therefore, you are constantly asking questions and listening to the answers, then acting or making decisions based on the new information, or, in a word, interviewing.

**How much interviewing do you do?**
Many readers will probably say that they do 'as little inter-viewing as possible', because managers from junior level upwards do not like interviewing and avoid it if possible. One senior manager I know still feels physically ill before she has to interview, despite the fact that her communication skills are well above average. She explains that each time she has to conduct an interview memories of her own painful experiences

1

as an interviewee return to haunt her. Paradoxically, her understanding of how interviewees feel should make her a far better interviewer.

This seems to be the crux of the problem. So many people have suffered from bad interviewing that they believe that the process itself is at fault, whereas in fact it is the interviewer's lack of skills that is really to blame.

## Where do you conduct your interviews?

You probably conduct your interviews in your office, but the real answer is *everywhere* – not only in your office, but in the passage outside, in the boardroom, the canteen, your car, on the stairs or in the lift. Ideally, as we shall see, your interviews should take place in a room where you will have no distractions; but this is not always possible. The fact is, an interview can be a success in practically any environment, provided you know what you are doing.

## How long do your interviews last?

To ask how long your interviews last is rather like asking how long is a piece of string – the answer is either 'it depends on the interview' or 'as long as it takes', but there is an important reason for asking the question. Interviews are generally either too long, in which case both the interviewer and interviewee become bored and lose track of what is happening, or too short, so that no real communication is set up between the two and no real information passes. For every interview there is a right and wrong length, and, as the title of this book indicates, one of the main aims is to help you to get the most out of each interview you conduct so that every minute is worthwhile.

## What makes a good interviewer?

Ask people what makes a good interviewer and you'll come up with a wide range of replies. I know because I've tried it; but here are some of the characteristics that are generally considered more important than others. Interviewers should be self-disciplined and self-controlled. They should be friendly, but not overly so. They should possess lots of empathy, but they must not identify too closely with others. Persistence and mental poise are also useful qualities to have, as well as tolerance and understanding. I have never met the ideal interviewer, if such a person exists. The good news is that, with training and experience, most mature individuals are capable of conducting perfectly adequate interviews, and some who possess a few extra qualities are able to hone their interviewing skills to a high degree of expertise. However, whether experts or not, the best always work to a system.

**How do you rate yourself as an interviewer?**
I have left the most difficult question for last. It is hard to tell how well or badly we interview, because we never ask our victims, the people we interview. If we were to ask, we might not like the answers we get. Speaking as an occasional victim in the past, I have been interviewed by some good and some terrible interviewers. I can remember one who conducted the interview perched on top of his chair, another who stood throughout gazing out of the window with his back to me. I have been asked irrelevant questions about my religion, my politics, even my attitude to sex – all, I might add, now subject to legal restrictions.

I assume that if you believed your interviewing skills were beyond reproach you would not be reading this book. The fact that you are reading it means that you think they can be improved – which is the best attitude to have. The worst interviewers are those who think that no one can teach them anything.
Most of us are never actually taught how to interview. We merely go from interview to interview making mistakes and hoping that somehow we shall learn how to do it properly. For those readers who fall into this category it is safe to say that you have probably picked up a few bad habits which, though not fatal, are not giving you the results you would like. If this is the case, the PQRSTU System will show you how to upgrade

the standard of your interviews so that they become more efficient and profitable for you and your organisation.

For readers who have no interviewing experience at all, the PQRSTU System will help you develop methods which you can apply to any kind of interview.

In Part One of the book I explain what the system is, and in Part Two I show you how you can apply it to some of the more difficult interviews you may have to conduct.

One of the greatest failings of management is the inability to communicate. Unenlightened management still believes that its main function is to give orders and to react if and when these orders are either not obeyed or not carried out as effectively as expected. Enlightened managers, on the other hand, know that their real function is to get the people they work with to share their goals and to work together to achieve them. The only way they can do this is to talk with them, not at them, to ask questions and to listen to answers – in other words to interview.

In the hands of the skilled interviewer, the interview is a rewarding experience for both participants. It is also a good way of getting noticed, because you can be relied on to choose the best staff and to motivate them to produce the best work. You will also have no trouble keeping them. On the other hand, clumsy, inept interviewing is very expensive, not only in financial terms, but also in human terms, because the wrong people are employed, the work does not get done, and unhappy staff are continually having to be replaced.

The quality of your interviewing, therefore, reflects not only on your reputation but also on that of your organisation, and the better you are at it, the greater your chances of rising to the very top.

# PART ONE
# THE PQRSTU SYSTEM

Interviewing is a large and complex subject and for this reason many managers find it daunting. What I have done is to reduce it to its basics with what I call the PQRSTU System of Interviewing so that the methodology can easily be comprehended by readers at all levels of interviewing experience. The PQRSTU System can also be used as a convenient checklist to enable the conscientious interviewer to confirm that all steps in the process have been taken, before, during and after the interview:

## P for Preparation

Defining the purpose of, and planning the strategy for, the interview.

## Q for Questions

Asking the best questions to ensure you get the information you want.

## R for Rapport

Establishing and maintaining a good working relationship with the interviewee.

## S for Skills

Prompting, probing and generally making the most out of the interview.

## T for Termination

Ending the interview in a positive and rewarding way.

## U for Unfinished business

Checking the interview's success or failure. Following up on matters arising out of the interview.

# 1
# PREPARATION

## $\boxed{P}$QRSTU

PREPARATION • QUESTIONS • RAPPORT • SKILLS • TERMINATION • UNFINISHED BUSINESS

A lot of people find preparing for anything apparently as ordinary as an interview a bit of a bore. They believe that preparation can actually spoil the interview by making it too formal and organised, and for this reason they prefer to let matters take their own natural course. Before I look at the advantages of good preparation, let me say that I have some sympathy with that point of view.

Over-preparation certainly can spoil an interview by destroying the element of spontaneity that will make it an enjoyable and stimulating experience for both participants. Interviewing at its best is a creative process that leaves inter-viewer and interviewee changed, if only in the slightest way and preferably for the better. Interviewers, however, who are so well prepared that nothing is left to chance find it difficult to be spontaneous and therefore they are not always able to respond creatively to the interviewee.

Good interviewing is also communication or else it is nothing, and this is not always possible if the interviewer is worrying whether or not the interview is going according to plan.

There are two extremes of interviewing. At the one extreme you have an interview that is left entirely to chance, in which neither the subject matter nor the questions have been

8

prepared in advance. The interviewer asks questions which come to mind or which the interviewee's answers have suggested, and that way interviewer and interviewee wander together from topic to topic in the hope that eventually something useful will emerge.

Psychotherapeutic interviewing is of this order. The therapist may either start with a question or leave it to the client to suggest a subject, and the 'interview' proceeds from there. However, as this is all done in the client's time and at his or her expense, it does not matter how much ground is covered, whereas most managers have to justify the time they spend in interviewing to prove that they are earning their salaries.

At the other extreme of interviewing is the highly structured interview in which questions are predetermined and answers are limited, so that neither party has much choice in what they say. In some market research interviews of this kind, the questions are written in such a way that the interviewer is required to emphasise certain words so that whoever is conducting the interview will always ask the question in precisely the same way. The interviewee's replies are also limited to 'Yes', or 'No', or variations on 'A lot', 'A little', 'Not at all'.

In recent years some organisations have taken to using structured recruitment interviews as a preliminary 'weeding-out' of candidates because they claim that it speeds up the selection process. This may or may not be true, but I suspect that the real reason is that the organisations cannot depend on the skills of their interviewers, and this is borne out by the fact that the interviews are programmed into computers, so that the candidate does not even have to talk to another human being.

Not that computer-programmed interviews are intrinsically wrong. Recently I sat with a computer for half an hour working through a medical questionnaire and in that time it learnt more about me, my habits – good and bad – and my health than most doctors (some of whom are truly awful interviewers) could in hours.

The disadvantages of the *planned* interview are none the less few compared to the disadvantages of the *unplanned* interview.

9

Unplanned interviews are:

- **Disorganised.** Where to begin, where to move to, what to talk about, all these questions are left in the air, so that the interviewer is half-depending on the interviewee to provide the interview with a purpose and a direction. The result of unplanned interviews sometimes is that the interviewee takes control. When this happens the interview is virtually at an end, because there is no longer any real communication between the participants.

- **Unfocused.** Without a pre-defined purpose, interviewers usually do not know what questions to ask or what areas to examine. The attention of the interviewees wanders and they quickly become bored while waiting for their interviewers to think up the questions.

- **Time-consuming.** The time spent in the unplanned interview is often far out of proportion to its results. What starts as a brief interview on a subject of relative unimportance turns into a long, tedious discussion because the interviewer is trying desperately to find a single topic on which to concentrate.

- **Uncontrolled.** A good interview resembles a lively conversation, and this is the way it should be, provided both parties realise that it is not (a theme that will be developed more fully later). The interviewer's role is essentially one of control, the interviewee's of response. When interviewers go into an interview unprepared there is the danger that they will lose control and whatever purpose the interview may have had will also be lost.

- **Emotionally overcharged.** With prepared interviews interviewers anticipate problems that might arise and so are ready to deal with them calmly and objectively. Unprepared, they are thrust willy-nilly into the maelstrom of emotions that can arise, particularly when sensitive personal matters are being dealt with. Unless they can reassert their control, the interview will collapse.

- **Inconclusive.** If the interviewer and the interviewee are uncertain why the interview is taking place, the chances are they will not reach any useful conclusions. Such interviews usually end with the interviewer reassuring the interviewee that, though they've not reached any decision, 'It's been nice chatting to you.' In truth, they both know that the whole business has been a waste of time.

Planned interviews, on the other hand:

- **Create confidence.** The manager who claims that anyone with a little commonsense can interview is probably hiding the suspicion that he or she might not be very good at it. It takes a certain courage for managers to accept that interviewing is difficult, that not everyone can do it, or do it well, and that some help may be necessary to improve their skills.

The reason for this is that interviewing is a highly unnatural and artificial process. It may look and sound like a conversation because it uses the conversational mechanism of question and answer, but it is not one, not even one 'with a purpose', as it has sometimes been described. Managers who avoid preparing themselves are, in effect, running away from the responsibility of conducting the interview to the best of their ability. They prefer to barge in and risk disaster than take the little time and care required to organise themselves properly.

If lack of confidence is a problem for you, the good news is that proper preparation will go a long way towards solving it. The more you have worked out in advance what you want to get out of the interview and how you intend to handle it to ensure that you do, the better you will be able to control and direct it to where you want it to go.

Interviewees take their cues from the interviewers, and if the latter appear confident and self-assured, the interviewees will also feel less anxious and more eager to help, so everyone wins.

- **Permit good listening.** Asking questions is only half the interviewer's work; the other half is listening to the replies. In Chapter 3 I shall be dealing with the importance of good listening in detail. For the moment let me say that it is almost impossible to practise good listening principles if you are not well prepared for the interview. Good listening requires an attentive mind, one that is focused on what the interviewee is saying, and you cannot achieve this if you are worrying about such basic problems as why you called for the interview in the first place, what the questions are that you should be asking and where the interview is heading.

It may also be that, because you did not set aside a special time for the interview, as you would have done had you been prepared, your mind is full of matters unconnected with it, and this, too, would get in the way of good listening.

A clear head is vital to the conduct of the successful interview, and it can be achieved only through forethought and planning.

- **Earn respect.** Interviewing is a two-way process. We, the interviewers, are judging the interviewees' performance, but at the same time they are judging ours. From surveys that have been conducted by various organisations on interviewing skills, managers by and large do not come out very well. Complaints are many, but most of them can be put down to lack of planning.

Much of the interviewing conducted by managers is with interviewees who are in a subordinate position to them, and so the temptation is not to take the interviews seriously. What such managers do not realise is that, by treating them as mere interruptions in a busy schedule, they are regarding their staff in the same light.

Interviewing is one of the core management skills, and it is not too far-fetched to say that the manager who treats every interview seriously and prepares for it properly, who conducts it courteously and efficiently, who does not waste time, who asks interesting questions and listens carefully to the replies is going to be a successful manager, well liked and respected by all.

Recruitment interviewing particularly involves people outside the organisation, so it should be regarded as an important part of public relations. If an interview is properly handled, the interviewee will regard the organisation itself in a good light; but if the interviewer is unprepared and wastes time, the interviewee will condemn the organisation as well as its representative.

The five steps to good preparation are:

1. Defining the purpose
2. Researching the subject
3. Organising the venue
4. Working out an interview plan
5. Preparing the questions

(The preparation of questions will be dealt with separately in Chapter 2.)

# 1. DEFINING THE PURPOSE

Every interview has a purpose. That is not nearly as obvious as it sounds. By defining the purpose, the interviewer also defines everything that follows, including the questions asked, the order in which they are asked, the special strategies that may have to be employed, and the final result. In other words, if you know what the interview is about, you know how to conduct it. If, on the other hand, you go into the interview without a clearly defined purpose, you risk wasting both your own and the interviewee's time.

Defining the purpose is usually a relatively simple task – at least on the surface. You know if you are interviewing candidates for a job in your organisation the purpose is to choose the right one. Think about it carefully and you will realise that there is more to it than that. First, you have to define the job, and second, describe the kind of person that will suit it best.

In some organisations jobs are vaguely defined. 'Personal assistant', for example, can mean different things to different people. To some it is merely a more acceptable title than 'typist'; to others it is a professional post requiring a wide range of skills. Until the scope of the job is established for both the interviewer and the candidate, any interview would be a waste of time or, worse, could result in employing someone who is either over-qualified or not qualified enough.

The purpose of some interviews is not clear at all and you may need to think carefully and do some research before you can identify what you want to achieve. For instance, Jane, one of your juniors who has always been punctual, has started coming to work late. You have given her a warning, but after a short return to normality she goes back to her bad ways. You decide that a disciplinary interview is in order.

However, after some research, you learn that she has recently suffered a bereavement, so the purpose of the interview now has to be modified into something resembling a counselling interview to help her come to terms with the bereavement. It may be that she will need outside help, and part of the interview would be to get her to recognise that need and accept the help.

What is the purpose of interviewing someone who is leaving the company? As we shall see when looking at dismissal and resignation interviews, it can be a very useful way of finding out more about the company from someone who no longer feels the need to guard their tongue. Organisations can also learn about management problems that might otherwise remain undetected. When, therefore, defining the purpose of such an interview, you would stress the information-gathering rather than the recrimination aspect of it.

Good interviewers are those who know what they want from the interview and organise themselves accordingly; poor interviewers are those who start without a particular end in view and spend most of the interview staggering blindly through it. It is not surprising that interviewees who have to suffer such interviews regard them as pointless and time-wasting and those who conduct them as poor managers.

## 2. RESEARCHING THE SUBJECT

Often interviewers go into interviews thinking they know

what they want to achieve and still fail. The reason is that merely thinking about it in a casual, unfocused way is not enough. More information is needed.

If, for instance, you are about to interview Stephen, an employee who has given in his letter of resignation, you would first want to know as much about his employment record as possible to determine whether or not you want him to stay. If his record turns out to be unremarkable, the purpose of the interview would be very different from what it would be if he were a valued employee whose presence would be sorely missed.

In addition to helping you define the purpose, preliminary research obviates the need to ask unnecessary questions and so saves time. For recruitment interviews, an essential part of your basic research is to read the candidate's application form, résumé or CV. Few things are guaranteed to irritate a candidate more than to have to give information which is, or should be, known to the interviewer. Your research may also include talking to people already doing the same or similar job, because it helps you to form a clearer picture of the kind of candidate best suited to the job.

Disciplinary interviews may produce hostility and resentment from the interviewee. For this reason, you have to prepare the ground for your accusations thoroughly by obtaining all the evidence of misconduct before the interview starts, otherwise you are in danger of having to defend your position against the interviewee's denials. This will lead you to become embroiled in arguments rather than remaining objective.

In short, then, whatever the nature of the interview, to ensure a clearly defined purpose some preliminary research may be necessary, but not so much that the purpose of the interview has been negated. If you can find out all you want about the subject more quickly and efficiently through other research, do so. There is no rule that says interviewing is the only, or even the best, way to achieve the results you are after.

# 3. ORGANISING THE VENUE

Interviews can, and frequently do, take place in the most unusual surroundings, in fact wherever two people can get together in relative peace and comfort. The word 'relative' is important because the choice may be limited and not always in the control of the interviewer.

For instance, the only place where a foreman can conduct an interview with a worker may be his office, but this will, in all likelihood, be noisy and, worse, exposed to the curious stares of the other workers, so that what should be a private discussion is seen, if not heard, by everyone passing the office. Similarly, interviews in open-plan offices are almost impossible to conduct in privacy. (When designing such offices, companies should always consider including a room where an undisrupted interview can take place.)

When choosing the venue, you should aim for:

- convenience
- comfort
- privacy

Also, the two essential freedoms should be kept in mind. They are:

- freedom from *disruptions*
- freedom from *distractions*

**Disruptions** come in many forms, of which perhaps the telephone is the most common and insistent, but is also the easiest to control. The problem is that many managers feel cut off and isolated if they are not constantly in touch with the outside world and so they cannot bring themselves to insist that their secretary holds all incoming calls. Sometimes the secretary will insist on putting calls through, despite instructions to the contrary.

Colleagues are next in the list of major disrupters. 'I know

16

the door's shut,' they say, popping their head round, 'but this will only take a second.' It seldom does, and, from the interviewee's point of view, the damage has already been done, because two things have happened: one, the interviewee's attention has been diverted; and two, by engaging in conversation with the intruder, you have sent out an unmistakable signal to the interviewee that he or she is of less importance.

In appraisal and disciplinary interviews, where the self-esteem of the interviewee is on the line, this second consequence might in the long run be even more serious than the first. You can always, with a little effort, redirect an interviewee's attention, but it is not so easy to restore confidence.

Ideally, at a good interview, both participants should be so intently focused on the subject under discussion that for the time being they forget the world outside. If the world insists on interrupting, the spell is broken and it may be impossible to restore.

**Distractions** are often more subtle than disruptions. It is possible to put a stop to phone calls and to deal with intruders quickly and firmly, but various kinds of distractions that occur in modern offices are more difficult to control.

*Noise* can come from a variety of sources – traffic, office machinery, air conditioning, even lighting – and there is not a great deal you can do about them except, perhaps, move to a quieter room. Certainly, if sound-proofing was inadequate, I would always avoid interviewing in a room overlooking a busy street. The problem is, of course, that on hot days if there is no air conditioning you either suffer the noise with the windows open or suffocate with them closed.

As a general rule, continuous noise, such as the low hum from air conditioning, is less of a nuisance than intermittent noise, and the interviewee, if concentrating on the questions, will soon ignore it. But irregular sounds disrupt the flow of communication as well as distract the interviewee who anticipates a repetition.

*Glare.* If possible, do not sit interviewees facing a window without a blind. The glare of the sun is very distracting, but most interviewees are too shy to mention it, especially if, as is usually the case, you are senior to them. They will prefer to suffer in silence, but the quality of their concentration also suffers to the detriment of the interview.

*Furnishings*. Thought should be given to the best environment for interviewing. If you insist on eye-catching objets d'art, you risk turning your interviewees into art critics who will spend the interview wondering more about the hidden meaning of the abstract painting on the wall than the meaning of your questions. On the other hand, a bare, characterless office is a dull environment in which to interview, and, in its own way, intimidating. It is not for nothing that a police interview room is a stark place, devoid of character.

If your office is bursting at the seams with furniture, books, papers and equipment and your desk is so cluttered you cannot find the papers you need for the interview, you are unwittingly signalling to interviewees that you regard them as an unwelcome interlude in your hectic schedule and that you would be glad to get the interview over with as quickly as possible. Your office tells interviewees something about yourself, so endeavour to give them a welcoming message.

I was once interviewed by someone who sat on the only clear corner of an otherwise crowded desk, while I was placed under an overloaded bookshelf in a rickety chair which he cleared of papers on my entry. Throughout the interview I was more concerned that the bookshelf did not fall on my head than with what passed between us, so for both of us it was a waste of time.

I have also been interviewed in a beautifully panelled boardroom. The only problem was that the panelling in narrow, horizontal stripes caused a 'strobing' effect, so that it was impossible to look at the interviewer for long without my eyes blurring, which proved to be a serious distraction.

*Chairs*. The interviewee's comfort is important if you want to ensure complete cooperation and attention, which means that the chairs should be neither too hard nor too soft. You don't want your interviewee dozing off! They should also be of the same kind and the same height. To show off your superior status by having a more impressive chair, especially one that permits you to sit higher than your interviewee, reveals a serious case of inferiority that will not escape an interviewee's notice.

The distance between the chairs should be from 1 to 1.5 metres. Closer than that and you will be crowding the interviewee, making it more an interrogation than an interview; further apart than that and the empty space between you becomes a barrier to good communication. Interestingly enough, in certain cultures with different ideas of what constitutes the individual's living space, a metre would seem to imply that the interviewer did not like the interviewee. But for most Europeans and Americans, anything less than a metre is considered too close for comfort.

Chairs should be placed approximately at right angles to each other. This allows you to look at the interviewees when you ask your questions and for them to look at you when they reply, but you are both free to glance away if you wish. If the angle between you is too wide, you cannot see each other properly and you will lose eye contact. Moreover, looking at interviewees through the corners of your eyes will give you the appearance of being shifty and untrustworthy. (The importance of eye contact will be discussed further in Chapter 3.)

*Desks* are indispensable to some managers. They are essential symbols of their power and authority. Without them they feel exposed. But desks create an imbalance that is contrary to the principles of good communication, like having one chair higher than the other. Desks also prevent the interviewer from having a clear view of interviewees' body movements, which could give useful information about what they are feeling apart from what they are saying. If anything, a small table between your two chairs on which to place cups of coffee and relevant documents is all you really need.

Increasingly for busy executives, interviews occur outside the office, in environments such as cars, trains, planes, restaurants

ants and hotel lobbies that, for all practical purposes, are outside the interviewer's control. Or are they? A restaurant, for instance, can be a very convenient place in which to conduct an interview provided certain precautions are taken by the interviewer: all part of the business of preparation.

First, it is important to choose a restaurant that is conducive to quiet conversation, which means avoiding places where the music is louder than the decor, or where the customers come to be seen rather than to eat.

Second, avoid a table close to the entrance, or on the route to the kitchen or toilets. A corner table is probably the best, because there is less chance of being overheard by other diners.

Third, choose the kind of food which requires little attention, so that you can give it all to the interview. Shellfish still in its shell or unfilleted fish is out. Alcohol is, of course, a personal preference, but this, too, should be avoided or taken only in small quantities. Rather than lubricating the dialogue, it is more likely to cloud the brain, yours and the interviewee's. One of the first interviews I conducted as a journalist was with a wily old writer who plied this young innocent with a tumbler full of gin. By the time I was half-way through, I was putty in his hand, and he deflected all the difficult questions I had been so determined to put to him, leaving me with a bland set of facts that I could have got from reading his entry in *Who's Who*.

A final point about interviewing over a meal: if you are of a nervous disposition, and cannot hold a knife and fork or pick up a glass without trembling, you are giving your interviewees an advantage — they know you are probably even more anxious than they are. In this event, it may be a better idea to eat first and interview later.

*When* you interview is just as important as *where*. In other words, the time of day can affect the quality of the interview. For instance, conducting an appraisal interview at five o'clock on a Friday afternoon is not going to achieve much, because both you and the interviewee are probably thinking of getting home and of how you intend to spend your weekend. Interviewing immediately before or after lunch is also not such a good idea. Hunger distracts the attention and repletion blunts the intellect.

# 4. WORKING OUT AN INTERVIEW PLAN

A bored interviewee is an unresponsive one, and boring interviews are those:

- that go on too long
- in which interviewers go over the same ground repeatedly
- in which interviewers appear not to know where they are going
- that are too rigidly structured
- in which interviewers ask irrelevant or banal questions

The way of overcoming all these potential problems is to work out an interview plan. This need not be very detailed, just enough to give you the confidence and security to know which direction to take in order to achieve the purpose of the interview.

Think of yourself as the driver of a motorcar and your interviewee as your passenger. Every time you interview, you are going on a journey together. Now, at first it may be quite exciting to drive along aimlessly, but soon your passenger is going to become uneasy, then anxious and bored as you meander through strange streets. Finally, if you still haven't found your way, your passenger will get angry. But because you are in charge and the passenger does not want to be left stranded, he or she will say nothing.

With a map, you and your passenger would have had a far more interesting, lively and enjoyable trip, with time even to take one or two small detours. Most important, you would have reached your destination.

An interview plan is your map, and you should work out in advance:

- what subject(s) you intend to cover
- the order in which you intend to deal with them
- the length of the interview

As we have already seen, the *subject matter* will be determined by the purpose of the interview, so you first have to know why you are interviewing and what you want to get out of it. If, say, the interview is to determine whether an employee is ready for promotion to a managerial position, you will want to go over a wide range of subjects including their ability to handle their current job, their skill in managing others, their ability to work under pressure and meet deadlines, and how much they want the promotion.

For some of the more problematic interviews it helps to write down the purpose, so that you can look at it, consider it and change it if you do not think it is correct. Just thinking about it may not focus it sharply enough.

It is also important that you work out the *running order* in which you will take each topic.

The order should have a logical progression, so that the interviewees can see the direction which you are taking. You should outline it for them before the interview starts. Avoid jumping from topic to topic, because that will only confuse them.

While it should be logical, the order should not be so predictable that the interviewees are not going to have to think hard about their replies. Lively communication is what you are after, not the dull repetition of known facts, so aim to keep interviewees interested by ordering your topics in the most challenging and involving way.

The *time limit* you set for your interviews gives them both shape and sharpness. Consider that both you and the interviewee are busy people, and if you know how long the interview will last you can concentrate your minds on getting the most out of it in that given time.

Interviews, therefore, should not be open-ended. On the other hand it is not always appropriate to stick rigidly to a time limit. It is essential that managers are accessible to the people who work for them. By being too mean with your interview time, you are giving your people the impression that you do not consider them important.

It is not possible to state categorically how long any particular type of interview should last. The length is determined by the purpose. Recruitment interviews seem to depend on the seniority of the recruit – the higher the level, the longer the interview. An American survey established that interviewers spend four times longer interviewing senior management than unskilled workers – no more than fifteen minutes for the latter, one hour for the former. I have been dismissed from a recruitment interview in ten minutes flat. I don't think they could have found out much about me in that time, but it was enough to tell them (apparently) that I was not suited to the job.

Counselling interviews may take the longest – usually up to an hour – because it is important that the interviewer does not rush the interviewee when talking about intimate subjects. In general, few interviews of any kind need last longer than ninety minutes. After that, both participants are going to be past caring and certainly not alert enough any longer to concentrate fully on the subject. If the interview is not concluded within that time, it may be better to continue it on another day.

Getting the timing right means getting the pacing right, too. Planned interviews are well paced, They have a strong sense of forward movement, of both participants working towards a mutually desired goal. Unplanned interviews, however, tend to meander. Interviewers spend too much time getting the interview started, then, realising that the time is passing, skip important subjects in their rush to finish it. A colleague told me of a job interview she attended which ended abruptly when, in answer to his irrelevant and discriminatory question, she told the interviewer that she had three children. He assumed wrongly and unfairly that this meant that she would not devote all her energies to her job. In fact, they were all living on their own, but in his eagerness to conclude the interview, he forgot to ask her their ages.

With proper planning you will also know how much time you have for each stage of the interview, from the warming-up to the termination. You will be able to cope with interviewees who are slow to reply by gently urging them along without confusing or upsetting them; and you will avoid the embarrassment of stopping half-way, not knowing how to go on, because your plan will have charted your course.

# 2
# QUESTIONS

## P⬚Q⬚RSTU

PREPARATION • QUESTIONS • RAPPORT • SKILLS • TERMINATION • UNFINISHED BUSINESS

Ten general observations can be made about the use of questions in an interview:

• Questions are the necessary link between the purpose of the interview and the results. So, if you have not defined the purpose, you will not be able to work out the right questions and accordingly will not get from the interview the results you want.

• To sharpen up your interviewing, you have to sharpen up your questions. If your questions are off the point, too wide-ranging or too general, you will waste a lot of valuable time and show little for your efforts. It is not enough that you get your interviewees talking, what is important is that they talk about the things you need to hear.

• Planning means going into an interview with your main questions worked out in advance, but the supplementary questions which arise from the interviewees' answers can be just as important, because they may reveal more about the feelings that lie behind the answers. By using your main questions as a guide you will be free to put supplementary questions that will add *substance* to facts.

• Every interview is different, even interviews for the same job, because every candidate and every application form or CV

25

is different. Interviewers who rely on a formula of favourite questions are treating interviews as a mechanical process instead of as a single, unique relationship.

- Questions are the interviewer's main method of controlling the interview. Without them, the interview becomes a mere conversation without direction.

- Within certain legal limits (in the United Kingdom the Sex Discrimination Act and the Equal Opportunities Act, which prohibit questions that discriminate on the grounds of race, gender and religion) you can ask more or less anything you want. This power should be used to encourage the interviewee to make the most of the interview, not to demolish the interviewee's self-confidence.

- Too many questions spoil the interview. Some interviewers believe that the best way to get information from an interviewee is to throw out one question after another almost without giving time to reply. The old rule applies: the more is less; the less is more. The fewer (but better) questions you put, the more information you will obtain; too many, and you will drive your interviewee to silence.

- Questions should be based on mutual understanding. They should be expressed in a way you *and* the interviewee both understand. Interviewing is not a quiz; it is not the function of interviewees to try to interpret what you are asking, and as they are usually too shy or too fearful to ask interviewers to explain themselves, they will attempt to answer what they think you want to hear. In other words, they will not be giving freely of their own thoughts and feelings.

- Just as every interview has a purpose, so should every question. You should never ask questions merely to fill up the time you have allocated for the interview. If you have all the information you need, the interview is over, whatever the clock may say.

- Whatever the purpose behind each question, you should, wherever possible, make this known to your interviewees. Questions about personal circumstances, for example, should be asked only if they are strictly relevant to the interview, and the more open you are with your interviewees, the more likely you are to receive their full and honest reply.

*In general, a good question is one which encourages interviewees to give you the information you are seeking and, simultaneously, motivates them to keep on talking.*

Questions have been variously described by different authors as open doors through which information flows, as signposts along the journey you and the interviewee take, and as tennis balls which you and the interviewee lob to each other. However you like to think of them, they are crucial to the success or failure of your interviews.

Interviewees who know the right questions to ask will usually succeed in getting the information they require.

It is for this reason that writers on interviewing go to considerable lengths to explain what kinds of questions are good and what are bad, and to help interviewers, they also provided long lists of questions they should be asking in different types of interview.

Useful though such lists may be, they also disguise the fact that questions are as personal to interviewers as their style of asking them. Some general questions may be appropriate to certain kinds of interviews, such as recruitment (discussed in Chapter 8), but formula questions produce formula answers.

Questions have seven main functions. These are:

- to encourage the interviewee to talk freely and openly
- to control the direction of the interview
- to assist the interviewee to concentrate
- to pick up points that have been overlooked
- to encourage the interviewee to expand and explain
- to get behind a mere recital of facts
- to achieve the purpose of the interview

The questions you ask should be:

- open, not closed

- short, not long
- single, not multiple

# OPEN AND CLOSED QUESTIONS

Sometimes also called direct and indirect questions, these are essentially the two main types of question asked in interviews.

The *open* question is one which requires the interviewee to respond in as much detail as possible.

The *closed* question is one to which only one reply is required: 'Yes', 'No', or possibly 'Maybe'.

The rule about these two types of question is simple: in general, open questions produce open answers, closed questions, closed answers. Note the 'in general' because, as with all rules, there are exceptions. More on this below.

To ask an open question, introduce it with one of the six Ws: *Why, When, Where, Who, Which, What*, as well as *How*. Asking open rather than closed questions is the best way to encourage the interviewee to answer in as much detail as possible, because, unless the interviewee is being deliberately obstructive, it is almost impossible not to give a full reply.

If therefore you are interviewing a candidate about his last job, your question 'What were your responsibilities?' is much more likely to produce a more detailed reply than 'In your last job, did you do this or that?'

## Other advantages of open questions

Open questions are less time-consuming than closed ones. 'What are your outside interests?' takes far less time to deal with than 'Do you have any outside interests?', because a positive reply to the latter can result in your having to go through a whole range of possibilities – 'Sport?' 'Er – no.' 'Reading?' 'A little', and so on – before you get the full picture of the candidate's leisure activities.

Open questions are more enjoyable to use. They make the interview less like an inquisition and more like a conversation. Moreover, they challenge the interviewee to think more carefully about answering them than closed questions, where a single word will do.

They show that you are taking both the interview and, more important, the interviewee seriously. Not only does it demand more time and effort to think up good open questions, but it also shows more consideration for interviewees.

Facts are not usually enough; the feelings that lie behind them are often far more important. Indirect, open questions are the only way you can properly reach these feelings. 'How are you managing with the new machine?' will get you a fuller and more useful response than the direct 'Having trouble with the new machine, are you?', because the worker's problem with the machine may have less to do with the machine itself than with the clumsy way their supervisor has handled its introduction. Only with open questions will you get to the truth. Closed questions, as the word implies, effectively shut it off.

Yet, despite the obvious advantages of open questions, closed questions are asked far more frequently. This is partly because they are seemingly more natural to us. They are what we generally use when we have a conversation in which we talk without paying much attention to what we are saying or, indeed, to what we are being told. Open questions require more forethought and, let's face it, in interpersonal relations (of which interviewing is a prime example) thinking is not something we like to do if we can avoid it.

The skill of asking open questions is relatively simple to master. Whenever you think of a closed question, for example 'Did you get on well with your previous employer?' which will elicit a simple 'Yes' or 'No', pause mentally and put one of the six Ws in front of it – 'How did you get on with your previous employer?' or, even more specific, 'What problems, if any, did you have with your previous employer?' Quite soon you will find that you have developed the habit of turning all your questions into open questions.

From what I have said about closed questions, you would be forgiven for thinking that they had no uses whatever and that you should never ask them. This is not the case. Closed questions can be used:

- when all you want is to establish facts. ('Your first job was with XY & Co.?' 'Yes.' 'And you were with them for . . .?' 'Six years.')
- when you are establishing a new line of questioning. ('We've dealt with your education, now let's turn to your recent work experience. Did you enjoy your work at XY & Co.?')
- when you want to get the interview back on course. ('Before we go on to that, I'd like to ask you, is it true that you walked off the job without asking your supervisor?')
- when you want to develop a theme. ('Can you take decisions on your own, because I'd like to put to you some possible negotiating situations that you might find yourself in.')
- when it is half of a two-part question. ('You know that our factory is in Manchester?' 'Yes.' 'How do you feel about moving home?')

## SHORT AND LONG QUESTIONS

A rule of thumb that applies to all types of interview is that interviewers should speak no more than 20 per cent of the time, interviewees the rest.

*Short* questions show that interviewers

- have prepared themselves properly
- know what they want to get out of the interview
- are conscious of time and cost

Good preparation enables interviewers to see the trees as well as the wood and to distinguish between them. Since they are conscious of time and cost , they have worked out precisely what they wish to achieve from the interview, and are able to go straight for what is important in the most precise way.

Short questions permit interviewers to move through the interview at a good pace simply because the interviewees are able to talk with as few interruptions as possible. This does not mean that questions should be fired at the interviewees in a brusque manner. That is mistaking discourtesy for efficiency, insensitivity for deftness. They should always be put courteously, calmly and patiently.

*Long* questions tend to be asked by interviewers who are

- anxious and lacking in confidence
- unprepared, or
- show-offs

**Anxious interviewers** abhor a silence. They feel that unless someone is talking, filling up the space, as it were, the interview is running out of steam and they have failed to do their job properly. So their questions ramble on until they forget what they are asking.

**Unprepared interviewers** spend a long time trying to explain the purpose of every question, hoping the interviewee will think they know what they are doing.

**Show-offs** are more interested in making speeches (which is what, in disguise, their questions really are) than finding out information. They develop their themes at great length before putting the question, hoping that the interviewee will be impressed by their fluency and grasp of the material.

Long questions are almost always a waste of time because most perceptive interviewees quickly realise that the interviewers are floundering. They either lose respect for the interviewers or become even more anxious than they were to start with. In either case, the result is to reduce the efficiency of the interview.

# SINGLE AND MULTIPLE QUESTIONS

Interviews should move from one topic to the next through a logical progression of questions. From each reply comes the next question, until the end is reached. The progression moves faster and more smoothly if interviewees can devote their thinking time to the answers, not to working out what it is the interviewer is asking.

Think of the interview as a jigsaw puzzle. Each question is a piece that fits into the puzzle until a complete picture is built up. If you try to put two pieces into the same space, all you will achieve is distortion. Questions asked *one at a time*, on the other hand, produce separate replies, the one adding on to the next, until the picture is complete.

**Multiple questions** cause confusion and slow down interviews, because the interviewees first have to work out what it is you want from them before they can respond. How do interviewees answer a multiple question such as 'Would you have time for more training, and do you think you could benefit from it?' if, in their present circumstances, they do not have the time for more training although they think they would benefit from it? A 'No' to the first part would seem to apply to the last and make them seem to the interviewer uninterested in developing their potential. A 'Yes' on the other hand might mean them overloading themselves, which could lead to problems.

How would an interviewee reply to the following appraisal question? 'Do you and your department head get on well together? Have the occasional drink together?' They may get on well together but they never drink together. On the other hand, they may have the occasional drink together, but have many disagreements. If the answer is 'Yes', which question is being referred to? Similarly, a negative reply would be ambiguous, so that the interviewer will end up with a false picture of the relationship between the two employees.

Many interviewees are confident enough to override the problem and give whatever answer they think the interviewers are after; but for more diffident interviewees multiple questions can be intimidating. As they are reluctant to ask the interviewer to put the question more simply, they will waste time trying to make sense of it and, moreover, give replies which are not a fair and accurate reflection of their true feelings.

In addition to the above, questions should be:

- relevant
- straightforward
- interesting

**Relevant** questions relate, directly or indirectly, to the purpose of the interview. Irrelevant questions go outside the purpose of the interview. In the United Kingdom, questions put to women candidates such as 'Do you intend to have any more children?' or 'Who looks after your children when you are at work?' or 'What does your husband think about you going out to work?' are not only irrelevant, but can also be the subject of a complaint to the Equal Opportunities Commission.

Relevant questions are 'need to know' questions. For instance, a man with an unusual name or a different accent from your own comes to you for a job. How much do you need to know about the place and circumstances of his birth before deciding if he is suitable?

The test is to ask yourself: does the purpose of the interview justify the question, and will the interviewee feel perfectly happy to answer it? If you cannot answer either question with an honest 'Yes', if the purpose can be achieved just as well without it, and if it may embarrass the interviewee, then don't ask it.

**Straightforward** questions should give the interviewee the opportunity to reply in an honest, open and straightforward manner. Trick questions and leading questions restrict the interviewee's freedom of reply. 'Were you popular at school?'

is a typically old-fashioned job-interview question that is still being asked to which only a very brave or foolhardy applicant would reply, 'No, and it didn't bother me a bit because I was getting straight As.'

Trick questions are designed not to learn more about the interviewees but to trap them into revealing more about themselves than, in their view, the interviewer is entitled to know. There may be circumstances when this is necessary, where, for example, the interviewee is deliberately evading answering a question that is germane to the purpose of the interview; but the relationship between managers and employees should be such that managers can explain their reason for asking the question and expect the interviewees to respond with equal honesty.

In an appraisal interview with his bookkeeper, the manager of the accounts department who suspects that the bookkeeper wants to leave for a higher salary asks, 'What would you do if a rich aunt left you a million pounds in her will?' Instead of asking about his or her plans for the future the manager has tricked the bookkeeper into replying, 'Give up my job immediately,' which, though honest, only serves to confirm the manager's suspicions and, at the same time, suppresses the bookkeeper's real feelings that he or she is being underpaid.

Sometimes, for the best of motives, interviewers try to put words into interviewees' mouths because they would like them to make a good showing. The temptation, however, has to be resisted. Interviewees must be given the fullest opportunity to make of the interviews what they can, even if this means they will fail. Only by asking straightforward questions which allow them to answer freely can this be achieved.

Some interviewees are less forthcoming than others, but you will learn far more if you are straight with them than if you try to lead them or trick them into answering. Only when the interviewee is reluctant to give you information that is vital for your purposes should you use all your interviewing skills to probe the information from them. (There is more of this in Chapter 4.)

**Interesting** questions make interesting interviews. Admittedly, some interviewees respond to questions more enthusiastically than others, but challenging questions can inspire even the least enthusiastic interviewee, whereas boring questions turn all interviews into tedious chores.

Boring questions are:

- Those where the answers can easily be ascertained from some other source, such as the candidate's CV or application form in a selection interview.
- Backward looking, that is dealing with matters that do not relate to the interviewee's present life. A typical example is asking the forty-year-old applicant to a senior management post to talk about his or her early school days.
- Repetitive. Interviewers who are too lazy to think up new, more demanding questions tack on a 'Why' to every answer. 'I enjoy travelling.' 'Oh, yes. Why?' 'Because I learn something new all the time.' 'Why do you say that?' and so on, *ad nauseam*.

# 3
# RAPPORT

## PQ[R]STU

PREPARATION • QUESTIONS • RAPPORT • SKILLS • TERMINATION • UNFINISHED BUSINESS

This chapter deals with the following topics:

1. What an interview is (and what it isn't)
2. A few typically bad interviewers
3. The (non-existent) ideal interviewer
4. Setting the scene – a few practical hints

## 1. WHAT AN INTERVIEW IS (AND WHAT IT ISN'T)

To understand what is meant by 'rapport' between interviewer and interviewee, we should first look at what an interview is.

Interviews are *meetings with a purpose*. Usually they are between two people, though there can be more than two present, as in a panel selection interview. Mostly they are conducted face to face, but telephone interviewing is becoming increasingly common, though less so for management interviews.

New technology is introducing new kinds of interviewing. Computers are being used as part of the selection process by a number of major corporations, and the time is not too far away when interviews will be conducted by video and satellite.

As we have already seen, interviews are preferably *for a specific, pre-defined purpose* which is, or should be, known to both participants. They are part of a process, never ends in themselves.

They are an essential part of the machinery of management. Information is gathered in order that it may be acted on. It is never gathered merely for its own sake.

Interviews are not static, rigid performances or quasi-dramatic presentations which allow managers to make speeches or, worse, interrogations in which they can exercise undue power over others.

Interviews differ from conversations in a number of important respects:

- Though, at best, they may sound conversational, they are *controlled* by the interviewers *through the questions* they ask and which the *interviewees are required to answer*. If, for some reason, they lose that control, the interview is at an end unless they can restore their control through one of the strategies mentioned in the next chapter.

- In conversations the participants are usually, though not always, known to each other, and the rapport is already in existence or can be readily created. In interviews, the participants may be meeting for the first time and it is the interviewer's responsibility to create a working relationship between them.

- Conversations are open-ended. They can go on for as long as the participants want them to. Interviews are *generally for a set time* and it is one of the interviewer's responsibilities to see that they do not run on over that time, otherwise they cease to be cost-effective.

- Like conversations, interviews can take place anywhere, but whereas conversations can be improved by convivial surroundings with other people present – in a pub or restaurant, for instance – interviews suffer from such distractions.

- In conversations the parties enjoy equal status, and their contributions are equal, but not so in most management interviews, where interviewees are subordinate to the interviewers. Yet, paradoxically, despite the power of the interviewers, the focus of the interview is always on the interviewees.

• A conversation can be discursive, covering a wide range of subjects, only the enjoyment of the parties determining its success. The interview has to explore the subject matter to the satisfaction of both, otherwise it has been a waste of time.

To sum up, then, an interview *is a meeting usually between two people face to face, generally for a set time, controlled by the interviewers through the questions they ask and which the interviewees are required to answer.*

From this it becomes clear that the interview is a highly artificial relationship which both participants find tense and stressful. Interviewees particularly are aware that, not only are they required to answer the questions put to them to the best of their ability, but that they are also 'on show', exposing aspects of themselves to the scrutiny, as it were, of the interviewers.

For these reasons, it is important that interviewers strive to put interviewees at their ease in order to get the most out of them. Unfortunately, this obligation is not always uppermost in the interviewers' minds.

# 2. A FEW TYPICALLY BAD INTERVIEWERS

'To interview as you would like to be interviewed' is the first principle of good interviewing. Most of us have been interviewees at some time or another in our careers, and most have been unfortunate enough to come across some pretty bad interviewers. Just to remind ourselves that nobody is perfect, let's put ourselves back into the position of interviewees and turn the spotlight onto interviewers who display glaring inadequacies. They are in no particular order of awfulness.

**Windbags** ask questions that seem to go on for ever, then, just as we start to reply, interrupt with a comment or another question. At recruitment interviews, they are so keen on selling us their own brilliance, the job or their organisation that they are not interested in listening to what we have to offer. When we do speak, their eyes glaze over with boredom, or they become fixed on some point in the room behind our shoulders, so that, if we haven't done so already, we begin to wonder what we are doing there.

**Bullies** fall into two categories. The first merely like to make us feel small. They are obviously troubled by a deep-seated sense of inferiority, but that is no consolation to us who have to suffer their rudeness. When we enter the room, they do not bother to put us at ease. Their questions are mainly closed, or if open invariably start with 'Why'. At the end they dismiss us with a wave of the hand. Mind you, we are thankful to get out of their presence.

The second category of bully is perhaps even more dangerous because they disguise their real motives behind some pseudo-psychological principle. They have heard or read about 'stress interviewing', and they excuse their bullying by saying that they want to see how we will behave under pressure. They throw question after question at us, and their body language conveys the clear message that they believe nothing we tell them.

They do not realise that it is questionable whether such techniques work. We may be able to respond well to a stress interview but collapse under the strain of a real-life crisis. On the other hand, we may find the environment of the interview such an effort that we freeze or clam up, but put us into a situation that demands all our emotional maturity and we perform brilliantly. No matter what our potential, we never get the chance to show what we really can do because we fail to come up to the absurd and unreal expectations imposed on us by such interviews.

This is not to say that interviewers should not make their interviews demanding. In fact, they have a duty to do so, but they can achieve this far more effectively by being polite and businesslike, by asking questions that make interviewees think and by giving them the freedom to respond fully.

**Runners** are those who would prefer never to conduct interviews, but as sometimes they are forced to do so, they try to get through them as quickly as possible, no matter how difficult or demanding the subject. Their eyes are seldom off their watches even while the interviewees are answering their questions. They also interrupt to make phone calls ('Just got to call my accountant') and brief excursions outside their office ('Have to tell my secretary something'). Invariably they end their interviews with a final 'Sorry, got to dash', and disappear out of the office before the interviewee has finished his or her last reply.

They probably do not intend to do so, but the effect of their impatience is to make us feel insignificant, and they very seldom get anything worthwhile out of their hurried interviews.

Good time-keeping is good interviewing, and if an interview can be kept short, it should; but that is different from forcing the pace.

**Neurotics** cannot sit still, physically or mentally. They pace up and down the room while we are trying to answer their questions. They twiddle with objects on their desk (of which they always seem to have an ample supply), they cross and uncross their legs, they make little paper balls out of our CVs, they bite their nails and examine their handiwork from time to time, and then cannot look us in the eye while they are talking to us. They also leap about from topic to topic, and concentrating on the direction of their questions is near impossible. After few minutes spent in their company we are exhausted and quite ready to certify ourselves.

**Policemen** are rigidly conformist in how they conduct their interviews, doing all the right things, but in such a way that they threaten us instead of making us feel comfortable. They will greet us and shake our hand firmly, but we shall not feel welcome. They will ask the right questions, but we shall not sense they are really interested in what we have to tell them. If we try to develop a point, they will interrupt with a curt 'Please, just answer my question', as if they were in a court of law.

They also sit in judgement on us, letting us know by the

occasional frown, the pursed lips or shake of head that they are convinced we are guilty, whatever we say. If we go before them for a job, we end up believing that everything we told them was a lie. When they appraise us, we feel that we are not worth the money they pay us. They never agree with us; but they are too well trained actually to argue.

**Clowns** were told that the way to put interviewees at ease was to tell us jokes. Either because they are so anxious themselves, or because they are totally lacking in empathy, they do not realise that someone working overtime at being funny can be far more embarrassing and disagreeable than a quiet, polite individual who gets on with the interview with as few preliminaries as possible.

The other problem with clowns is that their humour is often in poor taste. They make jokes about our names if they are at all unusual. ('That one's quite a tongue-twister, what!') They tease young interviewees with references to their looks or age. ('You don't look old enough to be out of school let alone coming to us for a job.') Women are made to squirm with embarrassment with facetious comments. ('What's a pretty girl like you doing applying for an engineer's job?' – a prohibited question, by the way, under Equal Opportunities legislation.)

Clowns, we are told, are irrepressible, which is a pity because they can do a great deal of damage to the reputation of a company, and no one will ever persuade them to change their act.

**Shoulders** are always there if we need someone to lean on or to cry with, and even if we would rather just talk, they encourage us to express our feelings by shaking their heads or clicking their tongues sympathetically and by murmuring, 'How awful it must've been. How terrible for you,' and the like. Shoulders are like bullies. They, too, use interviews as an exercise of power, but in a more subtle and, possible, more dangerous, way. They do not insult or hurt us, but they want us to depend on them, and in the final reckoning both undermine our self-respect.

Instead of helping us, they make it more difficult for us to solve our own problems. We come to resent this apparent concern as an unwarranted intrusion into what we regard as our own business, and so they do more harm to us than good.

**Don Juans** are a menace. They imagine that they are irresistible to women, and they treat every interview with a woman as a potential sexual encounter. Their demeanour is over-familiar and flirtatious. Their handshake is lingering, sometimes accompanied by a hand on the arm or back; their questions, often personal, are charged with hidden meanings. ('Do you mind working late in the evenings?', 'What would your husband say if you had to travel occasionally?') Their eye contact, instead of being friendly and intermittent, is lingering and persistent. They are seldom so obvious as to lay themselves open to a charge of harassment or sex discrimination, but everything they do or say reveals them to be basically contemptuous of women. Because their actions are intimidating, no one has the courage to report them, so they continue with their odious activities undetected.

The examples, admittedly, are slightly exaggerated and, though few people fall clearly into any one category, few of us are entirely free of some of these unfortunate traits. Awareness of our defects, however, is the first and most important step if we want to change ourselves because, in doing so, we shall also be improving our skills as interviewers, which is the whole object of the exercise.

# 3. THE (NON-EXISTENT) IDEAL INTERVIEWER

Interviewers have the responsibility to make the interview into the kind of meeting that, no matter how difficult it might have been for them, interviewees will leave feeling that they have been taken seriously and that the interviewers have valued the time spent with them.

To achieve this, interviewers ideally should possess some, if not all, the following characteristics:

- empathy
- objectivity
- tact
- politeness
- patience

**Empathy** is the ability to step inside another person's shoes, to know how they are feeling. It is a gift seldom found in the movers and shakers in our society, those successful executives who have focused all their energy and determination on the realisation of a vision. Unfortunately, they have a tendency to see those with whom they work as extensions of themselves rather than separate individuals. When it comes to interviewing, therefore, they are unable to put themselves in the interviewee's shoes, because as far as they are concerned they share the same pair of shoes and they own them!

Some people have problems with empathy, partly because they find it uncomfortable to experience the discomforts of others, and partly because there is power in not knowing. If we do not consider what others are feeling, it is much easier to be rude, impatient, aggressive, hostile or indifferent towards them.

Another problem some interviewers have is distinguishing between empathy and sympathy. Remember 'the shoulders'? They were the interviewers who enjoyed 'helping' interviewees with problems and often ended up making them worse. They do not recognise the thin line that separates the two. Empathy is *understanding* how other people feel, sympathy is *feeling* it and, in addition, wanting to do something about it.

Every time you hear a hard luck story and you reveal by what you say or how you look how sorry you feel for the interviewees, you risk losing control of the interview, and if you do that, you cannot really help them. Only by remaining objective, and through your questions letting them come to understand their own problems and how to solve them, can you help. (There is more on this in Chapter 9.)

**Objectivity** in the way interviewers treat interviewees is essential if interviewees are going to be listened to properly. Most interviewers like to think that they are fair-minded and impartial and that they give their interviewees a reasonable chance to do well. If asked, most would deny that they are prejudiced, because prejudice is an ugly word with an ugly history.

In the obvious sense of racial or religious prejudice this may be true, and if it is not, the law, in its wisdom, has seen to it that those interviewers who do practise discrimination are liable to prosecution.

However, if not actually prejudiced, most interviewers are to a greater or lesser degree biased. Bias is the convenient shorthand by which we go through life making mental notes on the things that happen to us and the people we meet whom we like or do not like.

'Never trust someone who wears a bow-tie,' a former employer of mine, a fair and decent lawyer in all other respects, warned me. I took it as a joke, until I realised that anyone who happened to wear a bow-tie whom he interviewed for a job, or dealt with as a client, was going to be marked down in his mind as unreliable, perhaps even crooked, and treated as such.

Bias gets in the way of establishing good rapport, because, even though we may not be aware of it, we express our negative attitudes in our gestures and our facial expressions, which interviewees, who watch us far more closely than we realise, notice.

The raising of eyebrows, for instance, the annoyed frown, the pursing of our lips or the tapping of a pen will be seen by nervous applicants for a job as an expression of disapproval, and they will either spend the rest of the interview trying too hard (and failing) to capture our approval, or will withdraw into themselves and ruin their chances.

What ideal interviewers cultivate is tolerance, the ability to hear what interviewees are saying without making judgements, without criticising or interjecting their own views or opinions. *Outside* the interview-room they might disapprove of men who wear bow-ties, but *inside* they look beyond the bow-tie to the man himself and treat him as they would someone with an ordinary tie or no tie at all.

In a sense, objectivity is an aspect of empathy, as are the other requirements of ideal interviewers, because all relate to the interviewer's ability to understand how their actions affect interviewees. Being *polite* is acknowledging that interviewees are just as important as we are; being *tactful* is recognising their unease or discomfort and not deliberately exacerbating it; being *patient* is realising the difficulties they may be having and allowing them time to give the best account of themselves.

Interviews, as I've said before, belong to the interviewees, not to us. Their purpose is not to make us feel better about ourselves, but to obtain information upon which we can act for the ultimate betterment of ourselves, the interviewees and the organisations we work for or represent. If we establish good rapport with our interviewees from the start, we shall achieve this purpose in an efficient and business like manner.

The idea that you bring to the interview your whole personality intact, that you cannot choose to separate those aspects of yourself that do not favour good interviewing principles, is (to use a current expression) a 'cop-out', a dereliction of responsibility. We all have weaknesses, just as we all have strengths. If we make the most of the latter and recognise our limitations for what they are – bias, prejudice, intolerance, impatience – we can go a long way towards changing those aspects of our personality that are getting in the way of our becoming more effective interviewers.

## 4. SETTING THE SCENE

This involves:

- greeting the interviewee
- breaking the ice
- the warm-up

## Greeting the interviewee

Contrast these two examples:

In the first, the candidate at a recruitment interview is kept waiting in a bare room, stomach churning over with nerves, with nothing to take her mind off the forthcoming interview. She is then called by a secretary who tells her where to go but does not accompany her. She enters the recruiter's office while he is talking on the telephone and is shown to a seat by a wave of his hand. She then has to wait long minutes until he has finished his conversation.

In the second, the candidate is given something to read, preferably information about the company he is hoping to join, while he waits in the comfortably furnished waiting room. He is met either by the recruiter or by another responsible individual and is taken to the interview room. There he is greeted with a friendly smile and a firm handshake, is thanked for coming and, most important, is addressed correctly *by name* by the interviewer, who then introduces himself. The candidate will feel positive not only towards the interviewer and the company, but towards the interview itself.

In the first case, the candidate will receive the unmistakable impression that she is an unwelcome intrusion in the busy life of the recruiter, who will have to spend far more time getting into the interview, simply because he has made so little effort to establish any kind of rapport with her. In the second example, the interviewer will be able to move immediately into the interview and progress at a brisk and businesslike pace because rapport has been created *before* the interview has begun.

Even an interview in which the two participants know each other tends to be sharper and more clearly focused if the interviewer establishes a good relationship with the interviewee *at the start*. If you happen to be on the telephone when your interviewee arrives, get off it immediately and in such a way as to convey the message that the interview is more important than the call.

As we know when we meet people for the first time, impressions are formed very quickly. We take in their appearance, posture, expressions and, above all, their attitude towards us. At the same time, their social antennae are picking up signals from us, and on this flimsy basis we decide how we shall behave towards each other.

In interviews the same thing happens, but because interviewees are in a subordinate position to us, they will adapt their behaviour to what they perceive our mood to be rather than the other way round.

We should want interviewees to see us as polite, friendly, businesslike and purposeful, Moreover, they should feel that they are in the confident and reassuring presence of someone who knows what they are doing. Nothing is likely to make interviewees more anxious than to feel that the interviewer is as nervous and as uncertain as they are.

## Breaking the ice

Depending on how you handle it, this can be 'make or break' time. Some interviewers feel that to put interviewees at ease they have to come over as friends. This is not necessary. Friendly, yes, but you are not their pals, and it is ill-advised as well as unfair to pretend that you are, because they may either overstep the mark and try to return your friendship – which you will resent – or become embarrassed and reject your overtures. Either way proper rapport will not be established and instead a chill may set in which you will have difficulty in overcoming.

Jokes, good, bad or indifferent, should be avoided. You are not a salesperson trying to persuade the interviewees to love you or your company. If you are friendly to your interviewees, they will respond in like manner. Treat them in an off-hand way and they will either withdraw into themselves or turn hostile.

Avoid all personal references, no matter how innocuous

they seem to you as a way of relaxing the interviewee. 'That's a nice tie/bracelet/ring' may seem to you a perfectly innocent remark, but the interviewee might waste the first ten minutes of the interview trying to figure out whether you are being serious or sarcastic.

Stay off politics. Interviews are to seek information, not to engage in discussion or, worse still, argument. You do not, nor should you need to, know what your interviewee's politics are, so you cannot be sure that a seemingly innocent remark may not upset or irritate them. It may also put them off wanting to join your company if they think that your politics are diametrically opposed to their own.

What, then, you may ask, can one talk about to break the ice that is safe and harmless? Well, in Britain, there is always the weather, but if you find this too boring, don't bother. Travel (but without criticism of government investment in the railways) and parking are reasonably safe.

Sport is fine, but only if you are genuinely interested and, more to the point, they are too. How many interviews start with the interviewer launching into a discussion on the latest cricket/football/rugby score, which stops only when the interviewee admits to knowing nothing about the game? Do not assume because you like a game that they will, too.

Ice-breaking should be kept short – sometimes only as long as it takes to bring the interviewee from the waiting room to your office. If the interview is with someone you work with, it should last no more than a minute or two. If you do not feel comfortable with chit-chat or you think it is inappropriate, dispense with it; but remember that often you also need to relax into the interview, so it helps you as much as your interviewees.

## The warm-up

'Would you describe yourself as a happy person?' was the first question put in a practice recruitment interview by a student of mine, and it has stayed in my mind as a good example of how *not* to start an interview, especially as it was followed by, 'How would you define happiness?'

What is wrong with these two questions?

If you said that they are too general, too abstract and, frankly, too difficult for most interviewees to answer satisfactorily, you would be right. They are also probably irrelevant and would take too long to answer. How do you define 'happiness', and how many people, if asked, would be able to say right off whether or not they were happy, especially if they were about to begin a recruiting interview upon which their future could depend?

Earlier, I compared interviewing with taking a passenger on a car journey. Just as you will have a more relaxed trip and a more enthusiastic passenger if you tell him or her where you are going and how you are going to get there, so you will have a more positive and less anxious interviewee if you explain the purpose of the interview and how you intend to conduct it.

The explanation should be kept brief enough to bridge the gap that exists between you by putting the interviewee in the picture.

Thus, for a recruitment interview, you might start: 'I thought we'd begin with your recent work experience, then your educational background and training, and then some questions about your general circumstances. Is that all right?'

For a disciplinary interview: 'We've had a complaint about the unfriendly way you are treating some of our customers. I thought we ought to talk about this, find out what the reasons are, and see how we can work out a plan of action so that we don't have a repetition of it.'

Once you have stated the purpose and general outline of the interview, your next step is to ask your first questions. It is important to get them right, because they set the tone and mood of the rest of the interview.

They should relate to the interviewees' personal experience, so that they can answer them with relative ease. The sooner interviewees hear the sound of their own voices, the sooner they will start to relax.

'Tell me about yourself' or 'Tell me about your last job' are still fairly common opening questions, but they are too generalised and unfocused.

Avoid questions which relate to feelings rather than facts, for instance 'How did you feel when you were not given a rise?' or 'What do you think about these new plans for the department?' These should be left to later in the interview when the interviewees have warmed up and are feeling more confident of themelves.

At any time, but especially at the beginning, avoid questions you should know the answer to from your research. If you start with 'How old are you?' when the answer is staring at you from the applicant's CV, you are saying that you have not bothered to look at it before the interview. Similarly, if you begin an appraisal interview with 'You've been working for us for – how long?' your interviewees know they can say goodbye to any genuine inquiry into, and understanding of, their current job situation.

Going into an interview without working out your first questions is a sure sign of carelessness or indifference.

To sum up, then, your first questions should tell interviewees that:

- You know the direction you want the interview to take.
- You are interested enough in them to have done some research.
- You know something about their circumstances, but you need to know more.
- You want to establish a rapport with them in order to make the interview a success.

# 4

# SKILLS

## PQRSTU

PREPARATION • QUESTIONS • RAPPORT • SKILLS • TERMINATION • UNFINISHED BUSINESS

Interviewing, as we have seen, is not a natural activity like a conversation, nor is it something you can merely pick up. Like learning to drive a car, it requires, firstly, an understanding of the basic skills and, secondly, regular practice. And just as after my first (fortunately minor) car accident my father insisted I immediately go out and drive so as not to lose confidence, I recommend that if you have a bad or inconclusive interview, do not let it put you off, but set up your next one as quickly as possible.

As interviewing is a process of communication, the two most important skills interviewers have to acquire are:

1. How to encourage interviewees to talk, and
2. How to listen

## 1. HOW TO ENCOURAGE INTERVIEWEES TO TALK

Most interviewees come to an interview to do well, to make the most of the time they spend with their interviewers. For this reason, interviewers start with an advantage.

Yet, despite this, so many of them lose it within the first few minutes and seldom regain it. The interview often turns into a wayward, unfocused, time-consuming 'chat' from which neither gains.

You keep interviewees motivated in two ways – by what you *say*, and by what you *do*, or put another way, by your *verbal* and *non-verbal* skills.

*Verbal skills* include not only *what* questions you ask (which we have already dealt with), but also *how* you ask them. Even the best questions if put badly will discourage or inhibit interviewees.

## Using your voice effectively

- Speak clearly. If you whisper, mutter into your chest or talk with your hand covering your mouth, interviewees may not hear you, and though they may ask you once or even twice to repeat yourself, they will feel too embarrassed to keep on doing so. The result is that you will not be communicating with each other as you should without either of you realising why.
- Do not shout. A loud voice is intimidating.
- Vary the tone. There is nothing more boring than an interviewer asking question after question in exactly the same way.
- Keep your voice free of any expressions of approval or disapproval. This may be particularly difficult in, say, a disciplinary interview where you may feel strongly about what the interviewee is supposed to have done, but it is essential that you do so otherwise you will not be able to conduct the interview fairly.
- Lighten the tone. A deep voice undoubtedly carries conviction, which is fine when you are making a speech, but this is not the effect you wish to convey in an interview, where your role is to receive information not give it.
- Make encouraging noises. Your interest in your interviewees should not only be implicit in the questions you ask,

but explicit. Respond, therefore, to what they are telling you with 'Mm-mmm', 'Uh-huh', 'I see', 'I follow', 'How interesting!'. We do this naturally when we are involved in an interesting conversation, but interviewing tends to make us self-conscious, so we sit in total silence. As we shall see later, silence can be used effectively to motivate reluctant interviewees, but if you remain silent while they are answering all your questions your interviewees will eventually become discouraged.

- Use prompting devices such as 'I'm not sure I follow', 'In what way?', 'How do you mean?' and 'Why do you say that?' to indicate that you want your interviewees to give you more information. To be effective, these devices should be accompanied by encouraging eye contact and facial expressions, as we shall discuss below.

- Avoid verbal 'ticks', such as saying 'Yes,' to whatever interviewees answer, or 'O.K.,' or 'I know what you mean.' They can become an annoying distraction.

- To sum up: Interviewees pick up messages from your voice. They can detect anger, dislike, lack of interest in how you express yourself without you even realising it. The only message, hidden or otherwise, that they should be receiving from the way you speak is that you are interested in what they are telling you and that you want to hear more.

*Non-verbal* skills include eye contact, facial expressions and body language. We shall deal with each in turn.

## Eye contact and facial expressions

Most of us would agree that being looked at is pleasant. Much depends on how we are looked at, but if the look is accompanied by a smile, we feel better for it. It is nice to know that other people recognise our existence.

We have an enormous repertoire of facial and head gestures. To understand other people's thoughts and feelings, therefore, it is not enough merely to listen to what they say, we also have to be able to read their expressions.

We look at people's faces more than any other part of the body, and we tend to look more often when we listen than when we talk. In interviewing it is essential that eye contact with your interviewees is maintained both when you ask questions and while listening to their answers.

Provided that it is a friendly and expectant look, interviewees experience your looking at them as a reward that they are doing well. If, however, it is accompanied by a scowl or frown, they will know that you disapprove of, or disagree with, what they are saying, and they will either shut up, start to mumble or lose track of what they are saying.

Interviewees do not always look at interviewers when they reply to their questions, though when training interviewees I always recommend that they should, because not looking can make them appear as though they have something to hide. As an interviewer, however, you should be careful not to judge them too quickly, because if they are shy they may find eye contact difficult even for short periods. This does not mean that they are dishonest or insincere. It means, though, that they might not be suitable for a job where they will have to face public scrutiny.

Interviewees will also avert their eyes if interviewers stare fixedly at them. Staring is intimidating.

Sometimes interviewers cease to concentrate on what the interviewee is saying and without realising it they replace an intelligent, responsive look with a blank stare. Interviewees recognise this and react to it by turning away. Unfortunately, they also turn their attention off and the quality of communication is adversely affected.

Confident interviewees will look you straight in the eye and continue to do this for longer periods than diffident interviewees; they will also blink less. But, again, it is dangerous to make too much of this when evaluating them, because, as Shakespeare put it, 'That one may smile, and smile, and be a villain.'

Our facial expressions say much about us, and observant interviewees can gauge how well or badly they are doing by how we look. We should cultivate an interested but non-committal expression, making sure that we do not express surprise, shock, disgust, anger or any other negative emotions when we hear things we might not like.

To be avoided therefore are the following:

- raising eyebrows
- narrowing eyes
- pursing lips
- grimacing
- frowning

However, just to confuse, raised eyebrows together with a slight tilting of the head can also indicate that we are listening intently. Used with a long, expectant pause, this can be a very effective message to the interviewee that we would like to hear more.

The one expression that we all like to think we can recognise and interpret when we see it is the smile; but in fact there are a number of different kinds of smiles, and not all of them send out positive messages. I have, for example, recommended that when you greet your interviewees, you should accompany your handshake with a smile. However, if that smile continues to sit on your face once the interview has started, it indicates you are not taking them or their replies seriously.

Your smile should always be appropriate to what the interviewees are saying. Smiling when they are telling you something serious and remaining poker-faced when they have made an amusing remark means that either you are not listening or you have misunderstood what they are saying. Either way, your reactions will confuse them.

Some people smile more naturally than others. If you are an easy smiler, do not overdo it because you may look insincere. If your natural expression is grave, try a little harder but not too hard, because it will also appear false.

Smiles, too, can hide hostility, and if your voice is raised and your body taut, the interviewee will not be fooled by your smile.

To sum up your use of eye contact and facial expressions, here is a *checklist*:

- Look at your interviewees when asking questions and during their replies.
- Look at them in a friendly but non-committal way.
- Do not let your expression reveal negative feelings of dislike or disapproval of them or what they have told you.
- Do not condemn interviewees if they do not look at you when replying, because it may mean that they are are lacking in confidence, not that they are hiding something.
- Do not stare at interviewees. It is intimidating.
- Smiling eases communication, but do not overdo it, and smile only when appropriate.

## Body language

This is the term psychologists give to the way we communicate with each other through our posture and our physical movements. Using a complex vocabulary of gestures we express our thoughts and feelings, and at the same time as we 'read' other people's gestures, they 'read' ours.

An awareness and understanding of body language aids interviewers in two ways. First, if you are aware of what you are doing, you can control the signals you are giving to the interviewees and ensure that they are conveying the right message; and second, you can observe and understand what the interviewees are telling you through their gestures.

A note of warning: individual gestures on their own mean very little and in combination they can be contradictory. Only when they are part of a consistent cluster do they carry any significant meaning.

## *Interviewers' body language*

The interviewer's body language should be saying:

- I know why I am conducting this interview.
- I am confident in my skills as an interviewer.
- I am interested in you.
- I want to hear everything you have to tell me.

To ensure these messages are being delivered to the interviewees as unequivocally as possible, you should:

- Sit comfortably in your chair in an upright but relaxed posture, feet close together. Slouching, drooping shoulders or legs splayed out in front of you indicate boredom.
- Look at your interviewees with an interested expression, leaning forward when listening to their replies. Do not gaze blankly into space, eyes hardly blinking – what a teacher of mine used to call 'Windows open but no one inside'.
- Avoid sitting with your head propped up by a hand, eyes half-closed. It's the classic boredom pose.
- Try to keep your body as motionless as possible. Do not fidget, doodle on your pad, drum fingers on the desk or arm of chair, click your ballpoint pen or chew your pencil – all these and more signal lack of interest.
- Keep your arms and legs uncrossed. Crossed limbs are a defensive posture which suggests that you want to block off information rather than receive it; and as the interviewees tend to copy you, they will also start to defend themselves with their arms across their chests and communication between you will be restricted.
- Keep your hands away from your face, especially your mouth, because, apart from muffling your speech, the gesture signals uncertainty, tension or even untrustworthiness. Do something useful with them like making notes. (Note-taking will be dealt with in more detail in Chapter 6.)
- Avoid postures indicating superiority, such as sitting with your hands clasped behind your head and legs crossed –

one adopted by men more than by women. Steepling the fingers in front of you is a confident gesture, but combined with resting back in your chair makes it look more like arrogance.

• Avoid other specifically male postures that have no place in an interview, such as one leg draped over an arm of the chair, or feet on the desk. They tell your interviewees that you are much too important and have far better things to do with your time than to listen to what they have to say. They also convey territorial possessiveness, that you are the master of all you survey – a statement I imagine you would not have to make, since most of your interviewees probably know and respect it anyway.

• In contrast, make more of placing your hand to your cheek, holding or stroking your chin, and tilting your head, all the while looking at your interviewees with an interested expression. These gestures say, 'I am relaxed but at the same time alert and involved, and I miss nothing.'

### Interviewees' body language

We take in information approximately four times faster than we speak; therefore, while interviewees are replying to our questions we have time to study and observe them and still not miss anything they tell us. Given a little practice, this should become second nature.

The postures of positive, confident, involved interviewees will be, to a large extent, a mirror of your own. They, too, will:

• be seated comfortably with their legs and arms un-crossed, their hands resting comfortably in front of them
• lean forward occasionally when listening to your questions
• have their eyes on you, looking away only when they are considering a question and formulating a reply

Tense, anxious and frightened interviewees will express their negative emotions in numerous ways, some that will be obvious to you, some not. They may: fidget, scratch, bite their nails, pick at their cuticles or the skin of their hands, or cover their mouths with their hands when they are replying, making it difficult for you to hear them properly.

When they feel threatened, they will cross their arms and legs, men at the knees, women at the ankles, clasp the arms of their chair or ball their hands into fists.

These gestures will be accompanied by the frequent clearing of the throat, answers preceded by 'umms' and 'ahs', and the uncertain pitch and wavering tone caused by rapid breathing.

When you observe any of these signs, it is your cue to reassure them. This you do by softening your voice, leaning towards them and smiling when appropriate, all the while maintaining encouraging but not threatening eye contact. Check also your own posture to make sure that they are not by any chance imitating you.

Interviewees also have ways of telling us that we are not doing our job properly. If, for instance, they stare as though in a trance it is not because they think we are absolutely fascinating, but rather that we are boring them. Similarly, if they look everywhere in the room except at us, it is clear that we are not getting through to them.

If you take your time to introduce a question, you may see the interviewee tugging an earlobe. This means, 'Thank you, I've got the point. Now, when is it my turn to speak?' And if interviewees move to the edge of their seats, lean or point their feet towards the door, they are giving us the message that they have had enough of our tedious questions and want to get out.

Our response to any of these messages is to start the communication process up again by (1) making our questions more relevant and challenging, and (2) talking less and listening more – which is the subject of the next section.

## 2. HOW TO LISTEN

Of all the non-verbal skills, listening is the most important. In fact, as has been remarked before, asking good questions and listening properly to the answers are really what interviewing is about. Do those well and you should never have any trouble with your interviews.

The problem is that most people are not natural listeners. Without wishing to get into psychology, which is not my subject, I suggest that this is because, when we are infants, in order to survive, we concern ourselves exclusively with our own needs and wants. We also have to make ourselves heard before anyone takes any notice of us, so we never really develop the ability to remain quiet and listen to the needs and wants of others. Whatever the reason, the fact is that we find it far easier to talk than to listen.

Listening is not, as some would have it, a purely passive process which requires us to do nothing more than sit and look at the speaker with a fixed expression on our faces, perhaps occasionally breaking the monotony by murmuring 'Uh-huh,' or 'Very interesting.' That is 'false' listening, something we all experience and, unfortunately, also practise at social gatherings.

'Real' listening is an active, participating, creative process that demands sensitivity and intelligence as well as plenty of practice. It is also a skill that executives and managers at all levels – indeed, anyone who is part of a team, no matter of what kind – should study and work at.

The good news is that to acquire listening skills you do not need any special equipment except two reasonably good ears, and you can practise anywhere – at interviews, at parties, in clubs, pubs, and with strangers on trains, who will not mind if you are not perfect.

## Real listening

Real listening involves:

- concentration
- discipline
- empathy

- self-effacement
- silence
- preparation and planning
- objectivity
- understanding
- pacing
- patience
- creativity

### Concentration
In interviewing terms, concentration means putting all other thoughts and considerations out of your mind except for what passes between the two of you. Interviewees are the centre from which the information flows and anything that interrupts that flow is to be ruthlessly put aside. It means, therefore, cutting yourself off mentally and physically from the world outside the relationship you have temporarily formed with the interviewee. It means thinking consciously of what the interviewee is saying, not of other questions or comments you wish to make when they have finished speaking. It means, finally, showing all this to the interviewees through your body language, expressions and gestures.

### Discipline
Thoughts, fragments of ideas, memories flit continually through our minds. Most of the time this is not a serious problem, but when interviewing it can mean that we miss something of vital importance, not necessarily a fact, just an expression on the interviewee's face that could make all the difference to knowing how a remark was meant and to how it should be interpreted. 'The foreman and I get on like a house on fire' said straightfaced means one thing, said with an ironic smile means exactly the opposite.

### Empathy
Why should the ability to put ourselves in another's shoes improve our listening skills? The answer is that, if we have

some insight into their feelings about being interviewed, we know that they need the best environment in which to express themselves. So, we make sure that the room is right, that the chairs are comfortable, that refreshment is provided, particularly if the interview will take some time, and that they will be able to talk to us undisturbed by telephone calls and interruptions for the whole length of the interview.

### Self-effacement

Good listening is not about selling ourselves; if anything, it is the reverse – making hardly any impression except that we are there for the sake of our interviewees. The test is that if they are asked half an hour after the interview to describe us, they should find it difficult to do so unless they know us well. All they should be able to say is, 'How should I know? I was too busy talking.' If, on the other hand, they are able to say exactly what we looked like, it usually means that we were talking so much that they had plenty of time to study us.

It could also mean that they remembered the flaming pink suit, the ostentatious jewellery, the cloying perfume or the after-shave more vividly than either our questions or their replies.

### Silence

Silence is not mere non-speaking, but the expectant silence of the listener who hangs onto the interviewee's every word and wants to hear more. It is accompanied by the correct body language (leaning forward, hand on chin, for instance), the correct expression (interested, engaged) and proper eye contact, not a fixed gaze at some distant point beyond the interviewee.

### Preparation and planning

If you know what you want to achieve from the interview, if you have done whatever research was necessary to formulate your questions and have written them out in the order you intend to ask them, if you have planned for coping with any problems that may arise, your mind will be free of worries and you can give your attention entirely to listening to what the interviewee says.

## Objectivity

Interviewees entering your office bring with them their accents, mannerisms, vocabulary and particular choice of words. Bad listeners hear an accent or note a particular mannerism and instantly form a judgement – sometimes favourable but usually unfavourable – about the interviewee. By contrast, good listeners focus on the interviewee as a whole person. They refrain from making any judgements until they have heard *what* the interviewee has to say, rather than *how* he or she says it. Only when the complete story has been told will good listeners make their minds up and then only respecting those areas that are relevant to the interview itself.

## Understanding

The silences that fall between words; the hesitations; the emphasis on certain phrases; the slight stammer; the shallow breathing; the occasional cough – these are a few of the many hidden messages that add richness of detail to the information which interviewees convey in the course of their interviews. Only good listeners have ears sensitive enough to hear them, because their minds are free of prejudice, free of random thoughts, free of outside concerns. They are able to sense how the interviewees are feeling, what fears or anxieties they are suffering and what hostilities or grudges they may bear, and they will be able to separate these from the words they use. Good listeners develop lines of questioning that relate to these messages and so get through to the truth.

For instance, a generalised complaint, such as: 'I don't really like it in this department, they're stand-offish,' may point to a more specific problem. The good listener's questions will uncover the problem and offer a possible solution.

'What do you mean, "stand-offish"?'
'Oh, you know, they make fun of me.'

'Why do you think they do that?'

(Pause.) 'Well, because I'm not very good on this new word processor.'

'Would you like more training?'

'Yes.'

## Pacing

Good listeners know that interviews are learning processes for both them and the interviewees. They know that only when they feel that they are seeing things as their interviewees see them will they have accomplished what they set out to do. They want their interviews to be cost-effective, but they know that if they move too quickly, if they rush ahead with one question following rapidly after another, they will miss much and waste the time they spend. So they pace them according to how difficult the subject matter is and how deep they may have to probe to get to the substance of it. They work out in advance at what point to start, how long to spend on each topic and how to develop the questioning until they achieve their goal.

## Patience

As has been mentioned before, we hear things at least four times faster than we speak. As a result, poor listeners tend to become impatient and interrupt with another question before the interviewees have completed their last reply.

Being continually interrupted is inhibiting, because interviewees think that their interviewers are not really interested in what they are saying. Good listeners keep a tight rein on their enthusiasm and let the interviewees tell their stories at their own pace.

## Creativity

For the interviewees, good listening can help to release their own creative energies. Through it they can grow and mature. This is the rationale behind the so-called 'talk therapies' – psychoanalysis and psychotherapy. People who come to us with problems do not necessarily want us to solve them – in fact, they would resent it if we tried – but by listening to them we help them identify the problems and find their own solutions.

Here is an example: Jennifer comes to you for her annual appraisal. After a few questions it becomes clear that she is fed up with her job but doesn't really know why. Through your gentle probing and careful listening, she expresses her frustration at being ignored by her superior.

'What attempts have you made to seek recognition?'
'None.'
'Why not?'
'Too embarrassed.'
'Do you embarrass easily?'
'I suppose so.'
'Might that not be the problem?'
'What, you mean she thinks if she does praise me I'd be embarrassed?'
'Could be.'
'I'd never thought of that. Perhaps, then, I should tell her that I'd like her to make a bit of a fuss of me.'
'When it's appropriate, why not?'

## Listening blocks and how to overcome them

Blocks to good listening are:

- tension
- bias
- indifference
- impatience
- verbosity
- preoccupation
- distractions
- misunderstandings

## Tension

Tension can fuzz up the brain almost as badly as alcohol. It is to be expected that interviewees will be tense, but if the interviewers share that tension it is as if they were in different rooms. Interviewers hear the interviewees, but not the subtleties, the choice of words, the changes in inflection, the pauses and hesitations that give real meaning to the interviewees' responses. Only calm, confident interviewers hear *everything* interviewees tell them.

If you suffer from interviewing nerves, there are a number of books and courses available on how to relax; but at the risk of repeating myself, let me say that the best way is to be *properly prepared*. If you have thought out your questions and your strategy, you can concentrate not on how nervous you are but on the interviewee, who is, or should be, the sole focus of your attention.

## Bias

None of us is free of bias. We all carry round with us views, opinions and attitudes based to a lesser or greater extent on prejudice. Bias can work both ways, against as well as in favour of interviewees. You may not like people with high-pitched voices because the bully at school spoke like that, therefore, as soon as the candidate with the squeaky voice starts to speak, you switch off and they stand no chance of getting the job for which they may be wholly suitable. Another less suitable applicant is more fortunate because they play the same sport as you, so you only hear their good points and are deaf to the bad.

To be a good listener – and therefore a good interviewer – you have first to recognise your prejudices and, second, to leave them outside the interview room. Hear what the interviewees are saying, not what you would like them to say, otherwise you will never give them, or yourself for that matter, a fair chance.

## Indifference

At least bias is an emotion – something interviewees can fight against if they have the determination; indifference is a blank, an emptiness where there should be a real person. Indifference is saying, 'I've heard this all before, so I've stopped listening.' Interviewees sense this by the way the interviewer slouches, by his or her drooping shoulders, monotonous voice and blank stare, and they will respond either by withdrawing themselves from the interview, in mind if not in body, or by becoming hostile. Whichever it is, communication ceases.

There must be a purpose to the interview, one that the interviewer believes in, otherwise there is no point in conducting it. Some organisations, for instance, insist on regular appraisal interviews, and in principle this is a good idea, because it shows that management is both interested and involved in their workforce. But if they are merely a formality, they are worse than useless.

Carrying out too many interviews in one day, with too short breaks between each, can seriously impede good listening. After the first three or four, it will begin to seem that they have 'heard it all before', which is unfair on interviewees who come lower down the list. I have even heard of interviewers who eat their lunch during an interview because they haven't the time to spare.

To ensure that all interviewees are listened to, interviews should be limited to not more than six in one day, and there should be a break of at least fifteen minutes between each one.

### Impatience

The more you interrupt, the less you listen. Anticipate the interviewees' reply before they have finished speaking and you could misinterpret what they have been telling you, but because you have stopped listening to them properly, you are not able to correct your mistake by the time you get on to your next question.

For busy, clever, successful executives, this can become a serious interviewing problem. They pick up points so quickly that, once they *think* they have got the gist of the interviewee's reply, they either jump in with their next question before the interviewee has finished answering the last one, or they stop concentrating and start thinking about something else. Either way, they cease to listen properly.

Good day-to-day planning will ensure that you give interviewees plenty of time to tell their stories. Exert control on your impatience by pacing your interviews so that they do not last too long or finish too quickly.

### Verbosity

Some managers like to hear the sound of their own voices and treat interviewing as an opportunity to make speeches. Others cannot bear silences and have to be talking continually, otherwise they feel they are not doing their job. Then there is a third group who suffer from an excess of sympathy and, instead of allowing interviewees to make mistakes, try to urge them along with comments.

Interviewees do not need our help. In fact, any help we try to give them will probably hinder them. Our job is to encourage them to project the best image of themselves by asking challenging questions. Good interviewers recognise this and train themselves to speak no more than 15 to 20 per cent of the time, then sit back and listen attentively for the rest.

### Preoccupation

Interviews belong to the interviewees. Not only should you leave your biases ouside the interview room, you also leave the problems you may be having with colleagues, bank managers, husbands, wives, cars, boats etc. You can listen properly only if you clear your mind of all other thoughts and make the interviewees the entire focus of your attention.

This means keeping your wits about you and not being over-prepared, because, if you have worked out in too fine detail how you are going to run your interviews, you may find that you have 'space' to think about other things, and will cease to concentrate on what you should be doing. Taking notes helps.

## Distractions

Interruptions not only break the pattern of question and answer, they also leave behind them thoughts and problems that continue to block our minds. Time is needed to get back into a listening state so that, even if the interviewees ignore the interruptions, interviewers may find that they are missing half what the interviewees are saying.

The best place for your interviews, therefore, is one which allows you to listen without disruptions. If, despite your precautions, you are still interrupted, summarise what the interviewee was saying at the moment of interruption and check that you have got it right before going on.

## Misunderstandings

Through bias we hear what we want to hear; through misunderstandings we hear wrongly or we jump too quickly to the wrong conclusions.

Maggie, a successful saleswoman, has gone to see her supervisor to ask for a few days off.

'Why?' he asks.
'I need time to arrange for a mortgage.'
'You're asking the firm to make you a loan?'
'Who said anything about a loan?' she snaps back.
'Well, that's what you really mean, isn't it?' he says.

Here misunderstanding has got in the way of accurate listening. The supervisor has heard only half of what Maggie has said and has supplied the rest himself which, as it turns out, is incorrect. The result is that either Maggie does not get her perfectly reasonable request granted and is going to feel resentful towards her superior as well as the company, or he is going to mark Maggie down as being unreliable with money.

The key to good listening is to let the words from the interviewees come through to you as they are, not as you *think* they are; and, if you are not satisfied that you have understood what the interviewee is actually saying, to go on patiently questioning until you are sure.

# COPING WITH AWKWARD INTERVIEWEES

Theoretically, there is no such animal as an awkward interviewee. There are only inept interviewers. Interviewers are in the driver's seat. They have to get the vehicle to its destination, and if they don't get there it is because their driving was at fault, not because the passenger gave them wrong directions or grabbed hold of the steering-wheel and tried to take over.

Interviewees are not required to read maps, and any attempt of theirs to seize control of the vehicle has to be firmly resisted, otherwise you'll both end up in a ditch.

However, as we shall see, some interviewees can and do make the journey a difficult one, and to recognise who they are is half-way towards coping with them. You will note that some correspond to difficult interviewers, and if two of them come together in one room, they may end up at each other's throats.

## Seven types of awkward interviewees

- Windbags
- The silent
- Defenders
- Attackers
- The impatient
- Neurotics
- The inarticulate

**Windbags** often start off as reluctant interviewees, but once they get started it is difficult to stop them. They take the simplest question and turn it into an opportunity for a speech. If their replies were witty and entertaining, we would not mind them so much, but, unfortunately, they are invariably dull and rambling. They seldom get to the point or, if they do, they repeat it again and again. Totally lacking in empathy, they neither realise nor care how much of our time they waste, and for that reason alone they have to be firmly dealt with. You have to curtail their obsessive talkativeness and yet at the same time maintain rapport with them.

**The silent,** though the opposite of the first, also waste our time and energy. Sometimes they are very shy; sometimes they are deliberately obstructive, but not having the assertiveness of Defenders (see below), they take forever thinking of their answer which, when it comes, is no more than a few words. Not surprisingly, closed questions are their favourites, and they will seldom elaborate on a simple 'Yes' or 'No'. Anger only makes matters worse. We have to contrive to get them to respond more fully without appearing to be badgering or forcing them.

**Defenders** are easy to recognise. The moment we start the interview they bundle themselves into a tight ball, legs and arms crossed, hands gripping the chair, knuckles white, lips tight, and they look sideways at us as though to say, 'I don't trust you.' Breaking through the barrier they have erected is a tough job, because they won't budge an inch or do anything to help. Like the silent, they will contrive to say as little as possible, or will answer every question with another question. Our task is to try to break down their defences without appearing to do so, because, if they realise what we are doing, they will become even more defensive.

**Attackers** look at interviews as a battlefield from which they have to emerge victorious. They give no quarter, yield not an inch. They sit far back in their chairs, their hands tightly clenched in front of them. They stick their chins out aggressively and raise their voices. They stare us down, as if to say, 'I don't like your questions and I'm not sure I want to answer them.' If they smile, it is not out of friendliness but rather grim determination to win at any cost. What they do not realise is that their apparent victories are a defeat for them and us, because the purpose of the interview is seldom achieved in the atmosphere of hostility they create.

Our best weapon is not attack, but reassurance. We have got to make them feel that we are not their enemy; that cooperation will save time; and that only together can we achieve what we both want from the interview.

**The impatient** are recognised by their crossed legs, twitching feet, fingers drumming on the arm of the chair. Their bodies lean towards the exit, indicating that they would prefer to be doing something else that is more important. They interrupt us with the answer to our question before we have finished asking it. They do, however, have a positive value by making it clear from their behaviour that we are taking too long to ask our questions.

Confident interviewers who know they are moving at the right pace will not be rushed into going any faster and will make this point clear. But they can destroy the self-confidence of novices who are trying their best to make their interviews a success.

**Neurotics** or, more kindly, the emotionally highly strung can be spotted even before they sit down. They walk quickly with a jerky step, shoulders stiff, their arms close to the side. Their handshake is cold and clammy. Out of nervousness, they sit down before they have been invited to do so, and they wriggle and fidget throughout the interview as though their chairs were on fire. Their hands are seldom still: their fingers pluck, pinch or pick at anything within reach – their clothes, arms, hands or legs. They seldom look us in the eye. When they answer our questions, they cover their mouths and speak in a low voice and when we ask them to speak up, they become even more flustered. If they laugh or, as they more usually do, giggle, it is because they are frightened, not because we have said something funny. Their twitching is catchy and after a few minutes in their company we find ourselves imitating them. For what ails them, reassurance is the best cure. (See below for more on this.)

**The inarticulate** are in one sense the most unfortunate.

Interviewing is communication; they know this as well as we do, but they are unable to overcome barriers of fear and anxiety to express themselves as fully as they would like. A vicious circle is set in motion: they struggle to reply to our questions, they become even more conscious of their struggle and so they become more inarticulate.

We have to break through this circle by listening with all our powers of concentration, even if time is limited. We must help them to tell their stories by guiding them with small steps, avoiding long silences, and as they talk to listen to clues that will give us the chance to prompt them to reveal more about themselves.

# STRATEGIES

Most interviewees, like most interviewers, are a mixture of good and bad, of awkward and obliging. They usually come to interviews in a positive frame of mind, recognising that it is in their own best interests to cooperate. However, even responsive interviewees have bad moments when for one reason or another they display some of the characteristics discussed above, so it is just as well to be prepared for them. Fortunately, we are not helpless in the face of opposition. There are a number of strategies we can use to overcome problems. The most important of all is:

## Reassurance

Reassurance is not really a 'strategy' as such because it is something you have to convey to everyone you interview, no matter who they are or what their personal characteristics. You have to show them that you see them, recognise them and respect them as individuals in their own right. More than that, you have to make them feel that, while the interviewing is taking place, they are the only people in your world who have valuable things to say and important contributions to make.

Reassurance comes from the moment you greet them and introduce yourself. They are also reassured when you explain the nature of the interview and the shape it will take, and when they hear the sound of their own voices.

Therefore, ask your questions, keeping them straightforward and, as far as possible, based on their own experiences. Ask, 'What did you do?' rather than, 'How did you feel?'

## Special strategies

- Probing
- Reflecting and restating
- Summarising
- Interruptions
- Silence
- Stress
- Ignorance
- Negotiation

### *Probing*

Phrases like 'interviews belong to the interviewees' may have given the impression that I believe interviewers should make life easy for interviewees; that they should ask easy questions, and pat interviewees on the back no matter how well or badly they answer.

Nothing could be further from the truth. Interviews should be hard work for both you and the interviewees. This is the only way their purpose can be achieved. So-called 'easy' interviews often create more work for interviewers because they have to set up more interviews to get the data that they did not obtain in the first one.

Our job is not only to listen, but also to penetrate the evasions, half-truths, clichés, asides and downright lies until we get to the truth or as close to it as possible, given that this is not an interrogation and we are not the police. We also have to watch the interviewees, checking to see that what they say fits their body language.

If the candidate tells you 'I enjoyed my last job very much' but their expression says the opposite, you have to probe to find out what they really thought of it and not stop there, but find out why. If, because of inattentiveness, apathy or laziness, you leave it unsaid, you may be losing valuable information, not only about their former job, but also about the candidate.

Clichés must not be allowed to pass without close examination, because they reveal far more about the interviewee's feelings than mere factual replies.

'What did you mean when you said about your last employer, "We didn't always see eye to eye"?'

All too often interviewers, especially those lacking in self-confidence, let interviewees get away with superficial responses to important questions. Their excuse is that they did not have the time, or that to have probed deeper may have embarrassed the interviewee, or they did not think it was that important *at the time*. To do your job efficiently, you must not let the interviewee off the hook. You have to probe and probe until you get an answer that will satisfy you.

'I meant that we had our differences.'
'What did you disagree about?'
'This and that.'
'Could you give me some specific examples?'

At the same time as probing, you have to reassure interviewees that you are *for* them, not *against* them, that your search for the truth is not merely out of curiosity or because you do not trust them.

This you do by turning negatives into positives: 'My life seems to be passing me by, and I'm getting nowhere', 'We all feel like that from time to time. What in particular is worrying you?'

By reinforcing the positive: 'I'm doing the best I can'. 'I agree. You're making a lot of progress.'

By using positive verbalisations and exclamations of approval such as 'Uh-huh', 'Mm-mm', 'I see', 'How interesting'.

By using gestures and body language to indicate total interest and involvement, such as nodding your head from time to time, leaning into the interviewee's reply, smiling when appropriate, stroking your chin, tilting your head.

### Reflecting and restating

Sometimes interviewees need a breathing space, a time when they can reconsider their statements and perhaps add to or amend them. Sometimes, also, they do not give enough information and the interviewer is convinced that there is more to come. To encourage interviewees to give you a fuller answer, restate their last reply, either the whole of it or just the last phrase or two. You can either repeat it word for word or paraphrase it in your own words, then give the interviewees time to consider their further reply.

'Things at home could be better. I think my wife's getting a bit fed up with me being away all the time.' (Pause.)
'Fed up.'
'Yes. You know, she says it's the kids.'

Restating loses its effect and becomes irritating if you keep repeating the interviewee's last remarks; instead, you should rephrase their statements.

'Your wife thinks the children miss you.'
'Not miss so much, it's just that they're at that stage, you know.'

When rephrasing, take care not to put words into the interviewee's mouth by suggesting your own interpretation of events. Interviewees have to tell things as *they* see them, not as you *think* they see them.

Not: 'You mean they're getting into trouble?' which is supposition and would stir up hostility: 'Who said anything about trouble?'

But: 'They would like to spend more time with you.'

This hits the nail on the head.

'Yes, that's just it! She thinks I'm missing seeing them grow up, and she could be right.'

By rephrasing, or what some writers prefer to call 'reflecting', you are, as it were, throwing back an incomplete image of the interviewees' statement which you feel is important enough to want a clearer definition. Hearing their words coming to them from you, they understand the need to complete the picture.

You can introduce your rephrasing with: 'You mean. . .', 'Am I correct in saying. . .', 'In other words. . .' as in:

'We let ourselves down, I think.'

'You mean. . ./Am I correct in saying. . ./In other words your results did not come up to your expectations.'

Restating can work wonders with silent or inarticulate interviewees who find it difficult to give more than a tantalising glimpse of their feelings, so long as you do not overdo it, in which case it becomes counter-productive; and if you put words into your interviewee's mouth, it can also yield misleading information.

### Summarising

This is one of the most effective interviewing tools at the interviewer's disposal, and should be used frequently whether or not the interviewees are giving you all the information you require. Summaries are signposts which help you to see where you have come from and where you are going to. If the interview is going off the track, a summary helps to put it back on again.

Summaries are a useful way of prodding diffident interviewees along by reassuring them that you have understood what they have told you so far. 'Let me see if I've got this right. After you left school you went straight into your first job as an assistant because you did not think further education would help you.'

Summaries also help you to pace your interviews if you use them when you end one section of the interview and before you begin the next. 'We've dealt with your education and you told me that . . .' (Give a brief summary.) 'Now, let's talk about your work experience.'

Summaries should be kept short and to the point. If they go on too long, they break the flow. Too many of them and you will bore your interviewees.

### Interruptions

In general, interrupting interviewees, even those who are going on rather longer than is necessary, is not a good idea. For one thing, you never know when they may give you some vital information; for another, as long as time is not a problem, by letting them go on you are showing them that you value what they tell you. Interviewers who are always interrupting interviewees because they are too impatient to listen seldom succeed in getting the information they want.

With windbags, however, you have to butt in, otherwise you will be sitting there all day and, worse than that, you will not necessarily achieve the purpose of the interview. You need not stop them in an aggressive or sarcastic manner, as that might only turn them against you and bring the interview to a halt. Your interruption should be calm and tactful. 'This is interesting, but before you go on I'd like to ask you. . .'

You can halt the long speech by breaking in with a brief summary: 'You've given me so much that I seem to have lost my way, so I'd just like to check what you've told me so far.'

Contrary to the impression they give, talkative interviewees are often those lacking in confidence, and once they start to answer a question, they do not know how to stop. One way is to distract them. This is done in three steps: first, you reassure them. 'This is very interesting.' Then you suggest, 'Let's come back to that a little later on.' Finally, you move on to the next question. 'I'd like to ask you about. . .' Instead of objecting, they will be grateful to you for interrupting and letting them off the hook.

### Silence

As a rule, interviewers and interviewees alike hate silence. This is understandable when you consider that interviewing is a two-way communication mainly through the medium of speech. Interviewers think that they have failed if they cannot keep the interviewees talking all the time; while interviewees find silence disconcerting and, if it goes on too long, very stressful.

In fact, silence can play a very useful part in interviewing, especially in encouraging reluctant interviewees to give fuller replies. The silence must be deliberate on your part, coming after the interviewee has given an incomplete answer to your question. It is vital that while remaining silent you look at the interviewees in an interested and expectant manner, eyebrows slightly raised, head tilted to one side, perhaps leaning towards them.

If you are looking away they will think that you have either forgotten what to ask next, or that you have lost interest in them. You cannot remain silent for too long or do it too often. A couple of times in one interview and for not longer than ten to fifteen seconds. More and you can fatally damage the rapport between you.

### Stress

Stress interviewing should be left to experts in the field. Much of it is practised more for the perverse pleasure of the interviewer than to test the interviewee's ability to stay calm under pressure.

Usually it is a waste of time. Knowing that someone can survive a stress interview tells you only that they can survive a stress interview. It tells you little or nothing about how they will act under real pressure in the job itself. It is also very difficult for a serious interviewer to switch from being nice to nasty and back again in one interview. The changes will confuse more than pressurise the interviewees.

Having said that, there may be circumstances when you have to use pressure to encourage obtuse or uncooperative interviewees to give fuller replies to your questions. The most effective method is to worry at a question like a dog with a bone until you get your answer. You do this by repeating the same question, changing it slightly every time, as well as by reflecting and restating (see above).

'How did you get on with your colleagues?'
'O.K.'
'What kind of relationship did you have with them?'
'We had our differences.'
'What about?'
'Mostly about budgeting.'
'Budgeting? Could you explain?'

Admittedly, it is hard work, but eventually the interviewees will get the idea that you will not let up until you are satisfied you have the information you want and, hopefully, they will start to cooperate.

Some interviewers who are bullies at heart believe that by firing big questions at interviewees one after another, they force them either to respond or to admit they cannot handle the pressure. Large questions receive short replies. If you ask a question that covers a range of feelings or experience you are likely to get a brief answer, because most interviewees are not philosophers or politicians and are not trained to handle major issues at one go.

'What do you want out of life?'
'To be happy, I guess.'

A vague question followed by an equally vague reply. If you have to tackle big issues like ambition, status, future plans, do it one small question at a time and you will succeed where bullies fail.

However much pressure you put on your interviewees, you should always remain fair, polite, even-tempered and tactful. There is never any need for rudeness, which is an abuse of power and seldom works. If the pressure is too great, interviewees will either crawl even deeper into their shells or walk out on you, so nothing will be accomplished.

### Ignorance

When interviewing experts on their subject, you should have done sufficient prior research to ask interesting and intelligent questions. Unfortunately, some experts assume the same degree of knowledge in others as they themselves possess and they glibly reply in the jargon of their profession, expecting the interviewer to follow them. When in doubt, clarify words, phrases and names that you are not familar with *at the interview*. Never attempt your own post-interview interpretations.

Ignorance, real or not, can also be used to probe for more information. Say there is a conflict between the foreman and a worker which is causing problems on the factory floor. You know from other sources that it started when the worker swore at the foreman but before you can solve the problem, you need him to admit it. At the interview, instead of challenging him about the incident (which he may deny), you can pretend ignorance so that he is forced to give you the full story in his own words.

'Might you have said something to Bill that upset him?'
'Perhaps.'
'Any idea what it could have been?'

Another version of this strategy is to introduce deliberately false information into the interview, thereby inviting the interviewee to deny and to give his side of the story.

'Is it true that you hit Bill?'
'I don't know where you heard that from but it's not true. I just call him a bloody . . .'

This technique is frequently used by journalists when questioning obstructive press officers whose function it is to give an official line.

'I understand the council are closing every school in the borough.'
'That's nonsense! They're only closing down two junior schools.'

### Negotiation

In recruitment interviewing interviewees are concerned to sell themselves and to make the best impression by answering your questions as fully as possible. But in problem-solving, counselling and disciplinary interviews, where interviewees may have something to hide, they can make each stage of the interview as hard as climbing a mountain, boulder by back-breaking boulder. You try probing; you try silence; you try pressure; nothing seems to work. This is the point at which either you tell them that there is no point in continuing, or you try negotiating.

This means that you step outside your role of interviewer and discuss with the interviewees why they are being obstructive. This, obviously, will require you to ask more questions, but you are doing so as a partner in a joint enterprise rather than as the controller of the interview.

'We seem to be getting nowhere. I wonder why.'
'You're asking me about things I don't want to discuss.'
'I can understand your reluctance, but you must realise that unless I find out what the problem is, I can't help you to solve it.'

Once the interviewees admit that the interview is making no

progress, remind them what you are both trying to achieve and how important it is that you do so together.

As with the other methods of probing that we have discussed, it is vital that throughout these negotiations you remain calm, patient and, above all, involved. Your aim is to maintain or re-establish channels of communication. Anger or indifference will drive interviewees further into themselves and you will forfeit what little rapport exists between you.

# 5
# TERMINATION

## PQRS⬚T⬚U

## COPING WITH PREMATURE BREAKDOWNS

Good interviewing is a creative process and as such it does not remain static but changes in tone and mood as it progresses. It can go from friendly to hostile, from cool to warm in a matter of seconds. How and why it changes depends on the participants, on the subject matter and on the purpose of the interview.

The artificiality of interviewing is borne out by the fact that two people, meeting possibly for the first time, are required to behave in a calm and civilised manner while one of them asks questions which the other has to answer about subjects that may involve feelings and facts of a private nature.

Interviewees can always refuse to answer, but it is usually in their best interests to forgo that right. So they endure the incompetence, the rudeness, the prying questions, because they reckon that they have more to lose by breaking off than by going on.

Interviewees are travellers about to set off on a journey and they bring with them backpacks or suitcases filled with emotions: anxiety, tension, anger, fear, hope. Not surprisingly, because of something the interviewer has said or done, or because the interviewee is feeling particularly vulnerable or edgy, these emotions may break through to ruin the rapport between the participants and, as a result, the interview comes to an abrupt halt. This interruption need be only a minor one, lasting a minute or two, or it can be a major breakdown that might turn out to be permanent. Either way, the responsibility for handling it rests on the interviewee.

Interviews also break down when the interviewee reverses roles and starts to ask the interviewer questions without being invited to do so.

'I notice in your application form you mention being in business for yourself. Would you like to tell me what happened?' the interviewer asks.

'To the business?' replies the interviewee.

'Yes.'

'Could I ask why you need to know?'

'Well, it is part of your past experience.'

'Yes, but is it really that relevant?'

If the interviewer permits the interviewee to continue in this way, he has lost control and the interview is at an end unless he can redeem the position in one of the ways suggested below.

Breakdowns happen to the best as well as the worst interviewers and they are always time-consuming and wasteful. Sometimes they occur spontaneously, but more often than not interviewees give warning signals. If you are observant and listen properly, you can anticipate problems before they occur and take the necessary preventative measures to ward off disaster.

The signs to look out for are:

**Eye contact:** minimal or, in the case of anger, fixed on you in a stare

**Body:** figeting; shallow breathing as though after a fast run

**Face:** jaws clenching and lips tightening

**Voice:** very quiet or hoarse

**Hands:** clenching and unclenching, either on the knees or, more commonly, on the arms of the chair
**Fingers:** scratching, feeling inside the collar, especially before replying, running through the hair
**Legs:** crossing and uncrossing repeatedly.

Signals do not come alone but are grouped together and, as the interview progresses, they will become more marked until the breakdown occurs. If, therefore, the interviewee avoids looking at you and at the same time clasps the edge of his chair, if he speaks in a low voice and also seems to have difficulty breathing, you will know that he is ready to explode.

In addition to *looking* for physical signs, *listen* to the way interviewees respond to your questions. If they:

- avoid answering certain questions
- avoid dealing with difficult and painful topics
- suddenly change the direction of their reply
- miss out important details in their stories

then, together with the bodily signs, you can be certain that the interview is causing them distress which they might not be able to handle.

Here are some suggestions for coping with breakdowns.

- **Analyse** what has happened that is causing the interviewee to react adversely. You do not have much time. Think quickly, make your diagnosis and take remedial action.
- **Keep calm.** Never lose your temper or respond to anger with sarcasm or insults. Interviewees usually have more to lose than you do. If they become hostile, remain friendly. If distressed, offer understanding. Do not try to solve their problems or act the psychiatrist. Your tone of voice, your facial expressions, your relaxed posture should also help to reassure and calm the distraught interviewee.
- **Be patient.** Give interviewees time to recover on their own. Tears or temper will only be momentary and if left alone

will pass; but if you intervene too quickly to try to make things better for them, you will only make them worse. The outburst may, in fact, be potentially healthy, because from it may come new ideas and solutions.

- **Remain objective.** After an outburst, interviewees feel awkward and embarrassed. Do not add to their embarrassment by insisting on knowing why. ('I'm really sorry about this. Is it something I said? I wish you'd tell me.') On the other hand, do not condemn. ('I don't know why you're going on like this. How was I supposed to know you'd just lost your mother?')

- **Distract** the interviewee by changing direction. If you have been asking questions which touch on feelings or on past experience that may be painful, stop and move into another line of questions. As a general rule, facts are less likely to cause problems than feelings, so ask a factual question. If, however, the subject that is causing the problems is important, return to it once the interviewee has calmed down.

- **Humour** can relieve most situations. Even though the outcome may be of great significance, interviews do not have to be deadly serious. As long as the interviewee knows you are taking him or her seriously, you can keep the mood light. The humorous remark made at the right time can go a long way towards diffusing a crisis. Make jokes against yourself, never the interviewee.

- **Depersonalize** the discussion. If the problem has arisen because you and your interviewee have become embroiled in a heated exchange in which you are swopping personal insults, get it back onto an impersonal basis as quickly as possible. 'What I think really isn't important. It's your views I want to hear, so shall we move on to the next subject?')

- **Postpone** the interview. When all else fails, and the interview has irretrievably broken down, you have little alternative but to postpone it. Sometimes, just suggesting it forces the interviewee to draw back from the brink and agree to continue. If this does not work, you will have to defer it to when both of you will be able to tackle it afresh. Less than efficient though this is, it is better to save time and money this way rather than 'flog a dead horse'.

- **Be on guard** and remember that prevention is better than cure. We not only have to keep the interviewing moving in the direction it has to go to fulfil its purpose, we also have to give our whole attention to what the interviewees are saying, to what they are doing and to what they are thinking.

# TERMINATING AN INTERVIEW

Interviewing, as I have said before, is like driving a car: the interviewer is the driver and the interviewees are your passengers. Both occupants know or ought to know more or less where the journey is going to start and where it will end, more in structured interviews, less in impromptu interviews.

Like unskilled, inexperienced drivers, some interviewers set their interviews in motion without knowing how to stop them. When they try to apply their brakes and nothing happens they panic and crash into the nearest wall. From the wreck, they and, more particularly, their passengers emerge bruised and shaken.

Skilled interviewers, however, direct their interviews confidently towards their destination, knowing that when their journey has reached its end, they and their interviewees will be left feeling that it has been worthwhile, but their time has been well spent and that they have gained something from it.

Endings are just as important as beginnings. We saw how it was necessary at the start of the interview to establish rapport with interviewees by putting them at ease and making them feel that they could trust you. Not only would the interview be more successful, but their attitude towards you and your organisation would also be more positive.

Similarly, at the end, the interviewees should feel good about themselves and positive towards you and the company you represent.

Again, it is a matter of putting yourself in the interviewees' shoes by asking yourself how *you* would like to feel after one of your own interviews. Would you like it if the interviewer seemed relieved when the interview was over and that he or she had already forgotten who you were by the time you got to the door? Or would you prefer it if the interviewer left you feeling that, whatever the outcome of the interview, he or she valued you as a human being?

It would be a strange individual indeed who opted for the former.

## A seven-point plan for ending the interview well

1. Signal that the interview is over by giving interviewees the opportunity to add any relevant points that may not have been covered and to ask you any relevant questions. This serves three purposes:

- Despite your preparation, you may have left out details that need to be dealt with.
- Interviewees should have the chance to speak freely and without pressure on matters of importance that are relevant to the purpose of the interview.
- Because they are no longer under pressure, their comments may show aspects of their personality that have not emerged in the course of the interview. In recruitment interviews, for instance, if they ask searching questions you know they are clear-thinking and have prepared themselves properly; if, however, they merely go over old ground, they may not be very interested in the job, or they may simply be unenterprising.

Do not let the interview drift into idle chatter. End it as soon as the additional points have been dealt with.

2. Aim to end on a positive note. This is not always as easy as it sounds. It is difficult to make people feel good about themselves if they have just been fired, but nevertheless they

should not be left without any sense of self-worth. It should be pointed out to them that they did not fit the job rather than that they were inadequate as human beings. (Chapter 10 has more to say on this.)

3. Be polite. Thank the interviewees for coming. If they are strangers, don't abandon them in your office building but take them personally out of the room, or arrange to have someone else to do it. If neither is possible, give them clear instructions how to find the exit. I've lost count of the number of times I have wandered around labyrinthine office buildings trying with growing annoyance to find my way out.

These small courtesies cost nothing but can mean a great deal to interviewees, because they affirm that, no matter how difficult the interview or how awkward they might have been, they and their contribution are valued. You overlook the public relations element of interviewing at your peril.

4. Be friendly. Avoid ending with recriminations and ill feelings, particularly with resignation or dismissal interviews. Whatever has happened to lead to this unhappy state is already in the past; it is the future that now counts, and as far as possible you should give interviewees the encouragement to believe that they can do better in the future than they have done in the past. It should also be your aim to leave interviewees with a positive impression of you and your company.

A story told to me by a colleague illustrates this point rather well. When he was dismissed by his employers they gave him a generous severance deal and a glowing reference. 'Why are you being so nice to me?' he asked his boss at their last interview. Swift as a flash came the reply, 'I'm worried that one day you may become a customer.' As it turned out, he never did, but he still has a soft spot towards the company.

In selection interviews, even if you know you will not be offering a candidate a job, you can still smile and shake their hand when they leave. You may also wish to interview them for another job more in keeping with their abilities on another occasion.

Some interviewers are embarrassed at having to turn people

down and instead part with remarks such as, 'That was a terrific interview. You did very well.' This raises the candidate's hopes unfairly. Far better to tell them at the time that they will not be offered the job but to do so in a pleasant manner, concentrating on the job's criteria rather than referring to personality.

Once you have done so, do not engage in any further discussion, otherwise you may find yourself having to defend your decision.

5. Do not leave interviewees dangling in mid-air. As anyone who has been through the traumas of an interview will confirm, the sense of relief at the end of the ordeal is soon replaced by a feeling of emptiness. You have done your best; the interviewer seemed interested in what you had to say; now what? Put interviewees out of their misery by explaining as simply as possible what happens next.

Recruiting interviews should never end with the 'Don't-call-us-we'll-call-you' routine. If you cannot make a decision directly the interview is finished, tell candidates how long they will have to wait before a decision is reached. Also let them know how they will be notified of the results. ('You understand that we shall be interviewing other candidates, but we hope to arrive at a decision within a week [or a month] and we will phone you [or write] to let you know.') Whatever you promise, stick to it. It is unnecessarily cruel to raise hopes of a prompt decision, then keep candidates waiting.

Problem-solving interviews should always conclude with the formulation of a plan of action. ('It's agreed then that you'll join the A.A. to seek help with your drinking.'); and at the end of a decision-making interview, a decision should have been reached which the interviewer or interviewee can act upon.

6. Knowing *when* to end is as important as knowing *how* to end. You should tell interviewees how long the interview will last or, in the case of counselling interviews, where you may wish to be more flexible, give them a general idea how long you need to spend with them. This is a necessary precaution to prevent interviews running on beyond their useful limits.

Some interviewers, as we have seen, find ending their interviews as problematic as starting them. Instead of finding a convenient point to stop, they allow the interviewees to ramble on while they struggle to keep their eyes open; or they chatter while the interviewees pray silently for a merciful release. When the end does eventually come, it is usually awkward and uncomfortable for both parties, who are left with the uneasy feeling that they made fools of themselves.

Interviewing is an integral part of corporate life and should be conducted in the same efficient and purposeful manner as meetings, negotiations and other business are conducted.

Interviewing is also part of a process, not an end in itself, so the work of the interviewer continues even after the interview is finished – as we shall see in the next chapter.

# 6

# UNFINISHED BUSINESS

## PQRST U

A post has to be filled, an employee needs help, decisions have to be made for which information is essential. First you decide on the purpose, then you prepare yourself, then you conduct the interview; then your real work begins. You have to choose the best candidate, or make changes to work practices, or dismiss a member of your staff. Interviewing, in other words, is not an end in itself, but is an essential part of a process.

The question now is: how much do you remember? Is everything the interviewee told you clear in your mind, or has it become a foggy blur? Do you remember whether she said that her reason for leaving her last job was boredom or are you confusing her with another candidate? What was it he said when you proposed that he move to another branch – did he like it but his wife didn't or was it the other way round?

How good, in fact, is your short-term memory or do you need notes to help you make valid decisions?

## NOTE-TAKING

There are two schools of thought about note-taking: those in favour and those against. Whether or not you take notes is your own decision, but to help you make up your mind, here are the main arguments for and against.

## Against taking notes

The main objection to note-taking is that it inhibits the essential forward movement of the interview. If, after every question, you have to ask interviewees to speak slowly so that you can note down what they say, you cannot maintain a momentum.

The second objection is that you lose eye contact. Unless you are skilled in the art of note-making, you are bound to have to look down while you are writing, which means that you are not able to give interviewees that necessary reassurance through eye contact that you are listening with interest and understanding to everything you are being told.

Thirdly, your own concentration, let alone the interviewees', can be seriously affected, because while they are talking you are busily engaged in writing, and by the time they have come to the end of their reply, you may well have lost your place in the sequence of questions and do not know what to ask next.

An argument for taking notes, as we shall see, is that without them your memory will be distorted by prejudice. The fact, however, is that even when taking notes you may be imposing a bias by selecting what you think is important and leaving out the rest.

The final argument against taking notes is a practical one: to make any sense of them, you have to transcribe some, if not all, after the interview, and everyone who has done this knows it is an arduous task. Even for a fast typist, it can take up to four hours to transcribe one hour of interviewing. Transcribing is a special skill that not everyone possesses, and for this reason, if for no other, many managers who do not have the right kind of skills or assistance prefer to rely on their memories.

## In favour of taking notes

Short-term memories are notoriously unreliable. A few gifted people have total recall, but most of us forget much of what we see and hear within a very short time. Notes are an invaluable aid, and you are in a far better position to make valid and effective decisions after the interview when they are backed up by your notes than when you are relying solely on memory.

Our memory is distorted by bias. We tend to remember only what we want to remember, which can work either for or against the interviewees. Because we took a liking to Candidate A, we can remember without notes most of the relevant details about her; but we have great difficulty recalling anything about Candidate B, because we did not warm to him at all.

The problem is multiplied many times if you have to interview seven or eight people every day over a period of over a week – a not uncommon experience for personnel officers in some firms. Without notes, it would take a phenomenal memory to distinguish one interviewee from another, let alone remember how they handled themselves. The chances of giving each a fair assessment based purely on memory are small indeed. The result is that you might end up employing the wrong candidate.

Note-taking is useful not only for selection interviewing but wherever it is important to keep some kind of record that can be referred to at a later stage. In appraisal interviewing, having the record of previous interviews can be helpful in deciding what areas of achievement or non-achievement to concentrate on, and what directions to move in. In problem-solving interviews, having notes of solutions arrived at allows you to judge whether or not they have been carried out.

The arguments for and against note-taking apply equally to tape and video recordings of interviews with, however, an additional argument against and that is the interviewees' right to privacy. Whereas few people would mind notes being taken of an interview, many more would object to having their words recorded on tape, especially if what they are telling you is of an intimate and private nature. For the same reason, interviews on video seem to me entirely wrong, even if they are with the consent of the interviewees, though I understand that some companies are now using them for recruitment interviews.

The presence of tape is no longer the distraction it used to be when the recording appliance was large and obtrusive; the presence of a camera certainly is. Candidates at selection interviews, keen to make a good impression, are usually very self-conscious. With a camera following their every move, their confidence will be destroyed before they even start. I hope the idea does not catch on.

If it is accepted that, at least for some interviews, note-taking is useful, if not essential, it is important to examine how best to take them so that you not only have an accurate record, but you also avoid distracting the interviewee and breaking the flow of the interview.

## How to take notes

- Always ask the interviewees' permission to make notes. They will seldom deny it, but it is only polite to do so. It is also your way of reassuring them that you do not intend to invade their privacy. If they seem reluctant, blame your need to do so on your bad memory.
- Keep them short. Take down only the points that you may need to refer to later. Verbatim notes are not necessary and, unless you are skilled at shorthand, you are going to have to make interviewees speak so slowly that it will become more a dictation session than an interview.
- Facts are easier to record than feelings. The latter require more thought and this might well distract you from the task at hand, which is to ask questions and listen to what the interviewees are telling you. You can, however, jot down your

own brief comments at the appropriate moments. (But see below.)

- Do not take notes when interviewees are emotionally upset. The knowledge that you are recording their anger or distress will only exacerbate the situation.

- For recruiting, use a standard assessment form wherever possible, as this will facilitate your note-taking and give you a much more accurate record of your impressions than mere random jottings.

- If you can't keep up with the interviewee's replies, put down a few words that you can add to after the interview, but at all costs avoid long pauses.

- After the interview, write up your notes as soon as possible. Add your impressions. Unfortunately, most of us cannot retain these in our minds for long, so the sooner you put them down, the better. If you are conducting a number of interviews in one day, try to ensure that you have sufficient time between each to complete your notes.

Note-taking is a skill that can be acquired with practice; so don't be put off by your first attempts if they are not a success. Having good shorthand or other speedwriting skills makes life easier, but if you don't want to learn, invent your own method, as do many practising journalists.

Good note-taking will ensure that all your interviews are properly recorded so that effective action or the right decisions can be taken.

Keeping a note of impressions of your interviews so that you can compare them with interviews conducted in, say, three or six months' time will also enable you to see how well your interviewing skills are progressing.

## SELF-EVALUATION AND VALIDATION

Interviewing has been described as an art, but that implies that it cannot be learnt – you either can do it or you can't. I prefer to regard it as a craft – one that with practice can be continually improved on.

Each interview we conduct should be a learning experience for us. We gain information not only about our interviewees, but also about ourselves. Prejudice, an inability to relate to others, lack of emotional stability, immaturity of judgement – these exist in all of us to a greater or lesser degree, but through interviewing we can learn how to overcome our weaknesses and reinforce our strengths so that, with time and experience, we become sharper, speedier and more effective.

Your judgement about interviewees is also an on-going process. Candidates employed after you have interviewed and recommended them can be judged against their future performance to see how accurate your predictions were. If, therefore, an employee turns out to be a success, you can congratulate yourself on the effectiveness of your interviewing. If, however, the employee has not come up to expectations, then, with the aid of your notes, you should identify where your judgement went awry and why the interview failed to reveal faults.

With appraisals, the goals defined and the steps agreed upon to develop or improve the skills of the appraised employee should be compared with what actually happens. Disciplinary interviews ought to lead to improved performance and it is your responsibility to check that this has, in fact, occurred.

# 7

# A CHECKLIST FOR FUTURE INTERVIEWS

## PQRSTU

PREPARATION • QUESTIONS • RAPPORT • SKILLS • TERMINATION • UNFINISHED BUSINESS

### 1

Go into the interview determined to make it sharper and more effective than any previous interview you have conducted.

### 2

Define your purpose clearly.

### 3

Prepare properly.

### 4

Write down your list of main questions and make sure they are mostly open questions to allow the interviewee to give you the fullest replies.

### 5

Organise the room so that there are no distractions and you will not be disturbed.

### 6

Arrange the furniture in such a way that you are able to maintain regular eye contact with your interviewees as well as observe their body language.

**7**

Make your welcome friendly and put your interviewees at ease.

**8**

Get the interview started in a brisk and businesslike manner by setting the scene, explaining the purpose and the order in which you are going to proceed.

**9**

Give interviewees an early opportunity to start talking about subjects based on their own experience.

**10**

Direct your body language, voice, facial expressions and gestures towards giving interviewees a sense of reassurance and trust.

**11**

Listen with complete concentration and a mind clear of all distractions, prejudice, bias and preoccupations.

**12**

Use encouraging verbalisations, nods of the head and phrases that motivate interviewees to give you a complete response to all your questions.

**13**

Pick up on evasions and gaps in the interviewees' answers.

**14**

Make interviewees work, not letting go until you are satisfied you have the full answer.

**15**

Use probing techniques such as restatement, repetition and silence to probe for the information missing from the interviewees' accounts.

**16**

Be polite and considerate even if you have to put pressure on the interviewees.

## 17

Maintain a steady pace, moving towards the conclusion but at the same time allowing interviewees time to give you detailed answers.

## 18

Handle emotional outbursts tactfully, remaining objective but understanding until they have passed.

## 19

Take notes without distracting the interviewees or yourself.

## 20

Finish within the time limit and make sure that interviewees leave with a favourable impression of you and your organisation.

# PART TWO

# THE PQRSTU SYSTEM AT WORK

In Part Two we shall explore three of the more difficult types of interview that managers are required to conduct: (1) recruitment, (2) problem-solving and (3) exit interviews, to show:

- how the PQRSTU System actually works
- how versatile and useful it is, and
- how it is guaranteed to *sharpen up your interviewing skills*

Approach the task in a systematic way and you cut your time and your potential for mistakes to a minimum. You also stand a far better chance of choosing the best candidate to fill the vacancy.

# 8

# RECRUITMENT INTERVIEWS

## PQRSTU

PREPARATION • QUESTIONS • RAPPORT • SKILLS • TERMINATION • UNFINISHED BUSINESS

Selecting staff is one of the most difficult jobs managers are required to do, and one that can greatly help their careers. Successful managers are those who can pick a good team.

Choosing the right people for a job is an onerous responsibility, because, if managers get it wrong, time and money are lost in wasted training, the unsatisfactory employee can disrupt other members of the staff and the cost in severance payments may be considerable. Understandably, for this reason, managers find the task daunting.

They go into the interview not quite sure what they should be looking for and, knowing that so much rests on their decision, they tend to be at least as uncomfortable and anxious as the candidates.

Personnel managers, who select staff on a regular basis, have the advantage over their colleagues who may only do it occasionally, because they have the benefit of both training and experience. There is no doubt that the more you do, the more proficient you get at it.

Interviewing is not universally held to be the best method by which to choose staff, and experts recommend that candidates also be put through other selection procedures, such as appropriate intelligence, psychological and technical testing, before decisions are made concerning their suitability. For instance, candidates for jobs that require addressing the public (such as training and public relations) may be asked to prepare and deliver a short presentation on any subject of their choice.

Interviewing is an artificial process. Selectors and candidates meet each other at the interview for the first time, usually only once and then for a relatively short period. Interviewers are expected to put aside their prejudices, their likes and dislikes that we all possess to some degree, and to choose the best candidate with complete objectivity.

Given such demands, it is little wonder that managers do not always succeed in making the right choice. Until now, however, nothing has been devised to replace the face-to-face interview as a way of selecting employees who not only fit the requirements of the job on paper, but are also of the right temperament to get on with their employers and fellow-workers with whom they will come into daily contact.

## Panel interviewing

Not all recruiting is done on a one-to-one basis. Much is conducted by boards or panels of interviewers, regarded by some writers as superior to the individual interviewer.

Panels allow more subjects to be covered in greater depth, because different interviewers can question the candidate on their own particular interests; and when deciding on the suitability of candidates more voices are added to the discussion and extreme views are balanced. On a practical point, panels allow for better note-taking, because when one interviewer is questioning, others can take down replies.

To many candidates, the panel interview is a nightmare, and unless they are very self-confident they feel defeated before they even start. In these circumstances it is difficult to establish a good working rapport, particularly if the panel is not being controlled effectively and members shoot questions at the candidate at random.

For a panel interview to work well, the team leader has to make sure that

- the team selected are compatible
- team members are each given a particular field to investigate
- they are allowed only a certain number of questions
- they keep strictly to a time limit

Team leaders act as Chair, controlling the interview throughout. It is their responsibility to

- greet and introduce the candidate to the other members
- provide the link between each successive interviewer
- ask any supplementary questions
- sum up
- thank the candidate for attending the interview

Thereafter, they are responsible for obtaining the views of the panel on the candidate and helping the members reach a final decision.

We shall now see how the PQRSTU System works in recruitment interviews.

# PREPARATION

- *Decide what the job is.* The more clearly you can define the requirements of the job, the easier it is to find the right person.
- *Write yourself a job description* which will include the following:

  - job title
  - the education, training and skills required to perform it
  - the day-to-day responsibilities
  - to whom the employee is responsible
  - the overall purpose

- the standards expected
- the conditions of employment
- the promotional prospects

● *Prepare a profile* of the type of person you are looking for who will best fit the job. Essentially, you are looking for someone who can do the job, who wants to do the job and who will enjoy doing it well. Identify not only the training and capabilities, intellectual and technical, that the individual should possess, but also the kind of temperament best suited to the job.

In addition, you should know in advance:
- how much energy and motivation they will need
- how much of an individualist or a team member they should be
- whether they should be followers or leaders, creators or decision-makers and so on.

Again, the more accurately you can define who you are looking for, the easier they will be to recognise when you meet them.

If the new employee will be working for you or will be a member of your own team, it is also essential that you feel you can work with him or her and that he or she will fit into the team.

● *Define the purpose* of the interview. This is to gain sufficient information about each of the candidates through the answers to the questions that you will put to them to enable you to assess their suitability for the job. It is also to find out whether the most suitable individual is willing to work on the conditions agreed upon between you and that he or she will enjoy and find satisfaction in the job.

## Planning

● Study the application forms or candidates' CVs, looking for information which will tell you which of them, on paper at least, is best suited to do the job.

• Carefully seek out any obvious gaps in their narrative (such as breaks in their employment record) as well as the evasions or hidden objectives that may make the difference between acceptance and refusal. For example, does it seem from what they write that they are applying only to encourage their present employers to raise their salary?

• Mark down any points that need to be explained, enlarged, or commented upon by the candidates. These points will make interesting and challenging questions to put to them.

• Work out the questions you want to ask the candidates. Think of the interview as completing a jigsaw puzzle. The information sent to you by the candidates together with any other details about the job form the basis of the puzzle, but there are still pieces that need to be filled in before the whole picture will emerge. The answers you hope will be given to your questions should give you those missing pieces.

• Apply, if necessary, to the candidates for documentary evidence of any of the crucial facts asserted in the application form. At the same time send out any available literature about your organisation relevant to the job.

• Choose the date(s) and place for the interview(s).

• Invite the candidates, asking them to confirm their attendance. If you have not had a reply from a candidate, check why not, otherwise you may find yourself wasting time waiting for someone who has no intention of turning up.

# QUESTIONS

Questions are what separate you, the interviewer, from the candidates. You ask them; they have to answer them.

Questions give you control over the interview and power over the interviewees, power that has to be used with great caution and only to the benefit of both you and the candidates.

Questions can be seen as sharp knives or as blunt instruments, but their main function is as invitations to candidates to give you as much information as possible so that you will not only suit them to the job but also suit the job to the candidates.

Here, then, are some useful *do's and don'ts*:

**Do:**

- Make a list of the main questions you intend to ask, but do not attempt to learn them off by heart. Keep the list near you so that you can refer to it when you need to.
- Jot down any supplementary questions that are raised by the candidates' replies. Don't attempt to keep them in your head, because you are bound to forget them.
- Frame your questions positively. Without neglecting the negative side of their story, your main purpose is to learn what the candidates can do, not what they can't.
- Keep questions to the point. Their underlying purpose should reflect the overall purpose of the interview – to find the right person for the job.
- Ask broad, open questions which allow candidates the freedom to show themselves off in their best light. Many candidates, especially if they are young and inexperienced, are by nature modest and find talking about themselves difficult. Give them the chance to shine.
- Ask closed questions only to establish facts or possibly as an introduction to a new topic. 'I see from your CV that you spent six months travelling in the U.S. Did you enjoy the experience?' Whether the reply is 'Yes' or 'No' you can then go on to open the discussion by asking for reasons.
- Remember the six Ws – *What, Why, Where, When, Who* and *Which*, together with the equally useful *How*, and train yourself to start your questions with one of them.
- Ask questions that will sum up what the candidate has told you. For example, to start the topic: 'Let's talk about your college career. What made you choose fine arts as your main subject?' To conclude before passing on to the next: 'Have I got this right, then? You decided on art because you thought it would be a good foundation for a career in advertising?'

111

• Ask all the questions that *need* to be asked if you are to obtain a complete picture of the candidate, even though they may cause him or her embarrassment or pain. The candidate's application form or CV may have raised some doubts in your mind about his or her suitability. You will have noted them down if you had done your preparation properly. Now is the time to clarify any evasions, so use it.

• Develop questions about feelings as well as facts – questions that inquire into what candidates *feel* about those aspects of life that are relevant to their work, for instance their attitudes to working with others, their expectations from the job itself. Facts are fine and necessary, but you need to know more about candidates than facts alone can tell you in order to make the right choice.

**Don't:**

• Start with controversial questions. Confronting candidates before you have had time to establish a rapport creates a barrier between you. A question such as 'Why do you want to leave your present job?', though perfectly legitimate, should come later in the interview when the candidate has had time to warm up.

• Ask anything that is irrelevant, which means controlling the urge to put questions out of curiosity rather than a genuine need to know.

In addition, *do not* ask any of the following:

• Multiple questions, that is, two or more questions at one time, such as 'Why are you applying for this job and what do you think you can bring to it?' They confuse candidates who have to work out answers to both at the same time.

• Vague questions, such as 'Why did you apply for a job with us?', which could mean 'Why did you apply for this particular job?' or 'Why this company and not another?'

- Blunt, threatening questions, such as 'How would you like my job?' instead of 'What are your ambitions?'
- Negative questions, such as 'Why were you given the sack by Blank & Co.?' Better to frame the question in a neutral way, for example 'What were your reasons for leaving?', and let the candidate explain the circumstances.
- Leading questions which force candidates to express views that are not necessarily their own but may be those of the interviewer: 'What is your attitude to the pernicious habit of clock-watching?'
- Personal questions that have nothing directly to do with the candidate's ability to do the job. 'What does your husband think of your going out to work?', 'Who'll be looking after your children?', 'What is your religion?', 'What's the origin of your name?' and so on.
- Discriminatory questions that contravene legislation on race relations and/or equal opportunities. Further information on these can be obtained from guides published by the Commission for Racial Equality and the Equal Opportunities Commission. See also the Institute of Personnel Management's Recruitment and Equal Opportunities Code. The Industrial Society also has a phone-in information service which deals with any matter relating to employment legislation.

# RAPPORT

Your task as interviewer is to maintain a balance between obtaining all the information you need to make your assessment of the candidates' suitability, and at the same time keeping them feeling relaxed enough to answer your questions in full, no matter how difficult they are. (I never said interviewing was easy!)

You only have a very short time to create a rapport between you. Here are *ten* necessary steps to take:

1. Find or create an environment that is friendly, non-threatening, conducive to concentration and free of distractions. Easier said than done, I know, but you should do everything you can to ensure that the candidates will feel comfortable (though not too comfortable!). Chairs should be of the same kind and height. A desk between you and the candidates is unnecessary, but if you feel unhappy without one, make sure it is clear. Photographs, executive toys and the like are a distraction.

2. If the candidates have to wait in a reception room, this too should be uncluttered and welcoming. Literature left on the table about your organisation for candidates to browse through makes a useful opening to the interview. 'Did you look through our latest brochures? Anything of interest catch your eye?' It also says something about the candidates. Those who have taken the trouble are likely to be more interested in the job than those who have ignored it.

3. Begin the interview on time, and ensure that you are well-briefed with your list of questions and all the relevant documents to hand.

4. Switch your mind off all other preoccupations and give your attention to the candidates. Though it may not loom large in your own career, the interview may well be the most important one in theirs.

5. Wherever possible, fetch the candidates yourself to the interview room, using the time to put them at ease with casual conversation about such non-threatening topics as the weather, travel, parking and the like. Don't forget to thank the candidates for coming. Politeness is cost-effective. The sooner you can get the candidates to relax, the quicker you can get the information and finish the interview.

6. Put aside all thoughts of rank and status while the interview is being conducted. They are immaterial. Your purpose is to find the right person to fill the vacancy, not to show how important you are. At the same time, you do not have to pretend to be someone you are not by talking to candidates in the same idiom as they may use. Not only is this patronising, it is also false, and they will see through you immediately.

7. Make allowances for nervousness. No matter who they are or how much experience they have had at being interviewed, most people are anxious when it comes to selling themselves. Do not be too quick to judge them if at first they do not respond freely and articulately to your questions. Be patient and give them time.

8. Treat the candidates as innocent before proved guilty. Though most will not volunteer embarrassing or awkward information about themselves, they do not go into interviews with the intention of deliberately deceiving the interviewer. They are sensible enough to know that even if they are not found out, lies or evasions will not help them in the long run.

9. People present themselves far better if they know what is expected of them and where they are in the scheme of things, so before you ask your first question, tell them what the purpose and shape of the interview are. They will probably know it, but it will help them to hear it from you.

10. Get candidates talking as quickly as possible. Some writers recommend warming-up with chat about subjects of mutual interest that may have emerged from reading their application form, such as playing the same sport, having the same hobby, living in the same area. Admittedly, these are natural starting points, but they also give those fortunate candidates who share the interviewer's interests an unfair advantage over the others.

# SKILLS

A good, working rapport with the candidates is essential; but that does not mean that you have to go out of your way to be nice so that they will think better of you.

More important than being agreeable is being professional. They will respect you more if you are properly prepared and know precisely what you are doing than if you ooze with charm or tell jokes, and they will respond accordingly by trying to give the best of themselves.

Unskilled interviewers give themselves away by:

- trying too hard to sell themselves and the job to the candidates
- becoming too involved in the candidates' stories instead of remaining objective and unemotional
- backing off too quickly if problems arise from questions they have put to the candidates
- accepting everything the candidates tell them at face value or overlooking areas that need to be probed
- overrating the inadequate and underrating the self-assured

To ensure that your selection interviews are tough, demanding, challenging but ultimately successful:

- Let the candidates do most of the talking – your own contribution should not be more than 20 per cent.
- Be systematic. Selection interviewing is essentially information-processing. You do not need to know *everything* about the candidates, only what is relevant to the job. Identify in advance the areas that need to be examined.
- Do not make too great a demand on yourself. If you try to do too many interviews in one day, you will cease to attend to what the candidates are telling you and start to anticipate what they are going to say next. This is unfair on them as well as yourself.
- Encourage and reassure candidates of your continuing interest by your manner – calm, friendly, objective; by your posture – comfortably upright in your chair, leaning forward into their reply; by your gestures – nodding your head thoughtfully from time to time; and by the way you look at them – non-threatening, interested, but not staring.
- Do not be too readily satisfied with candidates' answers. If the question is important (and all your questions should be, otherwise you are wasting your time), a full reply is in their interest as well as your own. Prompt gently but firmly by using

116

phrases like: 'In what way?', 'Why do you say that?', 'In what circumstances?', 'Tell me more about that', 'How do you mean?'

● Take notes without distracting the candidates, but ask their permission first, then wait until the interview gets going before you start. Take down the positive as well as negative points. It is discouraging if they see you noting down only their faults.

● Identify the statements that do not ring quite true or the gaps which need to be filled, and use rephrasing, reflection, summarising, repetition and silence until you get as close to the truth as possible, given the short time you have. Most candidates do not cheat, but many evade and more exaggerate.

● Do not condemn candidates for their faults – that is not your function. If an episode reflects poorly on them, try to see it from their point of view; but at the same time find out why they think the incident occurred, what their role was, and, most important, what they learned from it. We all make mistakes. It is what we learn from them that is the best indication of our strengths and weaknesses.

● Listen sensitively to their voices and, while listening, watch gestures, expressions and mannerisms to learn as much as you can about the candidates.

● Probe not only for failure, but also for success. Modesty sometimes prevents candidates from giving you the full story. Ask questions that show them off in the best possible light, and whether the episode reflects well or badly, put it into perspective. The complete picture is what you are after; minor details may distort it unfavourably.

# TERMINATION

To be a success, your interview has to be a two-way process. The information goes from the candidates to you and from you back again to the candidates. They tell you about themselves, you convey information about the job and the company, and possibly, if you are going to be their immediate boss, yourself.

How does this work if, for most of the time, you have been asking questions which they have been answering? When do they get the chance to ask the questions?

There is a school of thought which says that candidates should be encouraged to put questions to the interviewer throughout the interview and that this is the only way real communication can be established. The more conventional view, however, is that this makes control impossible, and that the interview will end up being a conversation without any direction.

The answer depends on how confident you are. If you feel you can handle interruptions during the interview and still maintain control, then it is a good idea to give the candidates the chance to ask questions. If you do not want to answer immediately you can always suggest they ask them later. But if you feel that interviewing is difficult enough as it is, stick to the conventional method, which is to leave questions till just before you close.

Either way, you should be prepared to answer them if you want to be certain that the person you pick for the job in turn picks you. The important factual details about your organisation, the job itself, its duties and location, the kind of person required and, of course, the benefits should be in the press advertisement or in the data you send the candidates at the time of applying.

In addition to this, potentially suitable candidates will also want to know:

- why the job has fallen vacant and whether the previous holder has resigned, retired, been dismissed or promoted
- what training they will require and how long it will take
- for whom they would work and over whom they would have responsibility
- what the opportunities are for advancement

Senior appointees might like to know details about the company itself that are not generally available, such as its growth over recent years and its potential for further growth.

Questions having been asked and answered, signal the candidates that the end is approaching by summarising and picking up points that you may have missed. It may also help to get the candidates to sum up their impression of the interview. 'From what we talked about, how do you see yourself in the job?'

Candidates will probably be as relieved as you to know that the interview is about to end, because they will want to get on with their lives. If you have done your job properly, they should feel drained but at the same time reasonably pleased with themselves. They should not feel that they are useless and worthless.

Thank them for coming, tell them that you enjoyed talking to them and found what they told you interesting. Get out of your chair, walk them to the door and shake their hand. It is demeaning to be dismissed by an interviewer with no more than a brusque 'thank you', or by one who continues writing notes without looking up or, worse, bids them send in the next candidate.

Do not, however, go to the other extreme and leave candidates thinking that the job is 'in the bag'. Do not tell them how well they performed or express the view that they have nothing to worry about.

Whether or not they will get the job, candidates have the added anxiety of not knowing. We have all been through it, yet regrettably some interviewers forget how unpleasant the waiting period can be. Do as you would be done by. Relieve them of some of their anxiety by telling them when and how – by letter, telephone or both – they will be told of your decision. If possible, make that sooner not later. And keep your promise.

If, by the end of the interview, you have made up your mind that, for whatever reason, the candidate is not suitable, say so in the kindest way possible. Indicate that the unsuitability lies with the job rather than the candidate, for instance, 'I'm afraid that the job demands more training or experience than you've actually got,' or 'I don't believe the job will challenge you or exploit your abilities to the full.'

Rejection is painful however it is conveyed, but at least the candidate will know where he or she stands and can apply for other jobs.

Finally, if you have offered to pay candidates' expenses for attending the interview, it is embarrassing for them to have to remind you or go through complicated bureaucratic procedures to get their money. Make sure they are paid promptly and with the minimum of fuss. Remember, their time is as valuable as your own.

# UNFINISHED BUSINESS

The difference between interviewers and candidates after the interview is that candidates have done their work. For interviewers the most important work still remains to be done, namely, choosing the right applicant.

Half the problem of making the choice is the danger of relying on irrational judgements based on superficial impressions of the candidate; the other half is finding a system that will give you the approximation of a scientific and rational decision.

Survey after survey of selection procedures reveal that the majority of decisions about a candidate are made within a few minutes of the start of the interview and that they are based almost entirely on irrelevant data. The rest of the interview is spent asking questions that will fit into these first impressions. The better the impression, the easier and more helpful the questions; the worse the impression, the harder the questions.

It therefore behoves interviewers – if they wish to be fair to all – to avoid making judgements until *after* the candidates have left the room. Then it is perfectly natural to ask yourself (or your fellow-panellists) what your impressions were. After all, you have just spent up to an hour in the candidate's company, going over his or her life story, learning the good points and the not-so-good. But don't stop there. Ask yourself: Why did I like or dislike the candidate?

Perhaps it was the voice that irritated you, or the way of sitting, or the nail-biting or constant sniffing. It may have been the hair or clothes – by themselves insignificant details but adding up to an unfavourable impression.

Just as important is to ask yourself why you *liked* the candidate. Beware, though, of what is known as the 'halo effect', where the interviewer gives a general 'Yes' vote to a candidate based on one favourable, and often not very important, detail. You may, for instance, share a liking for the cinema, or even a particular film, and, if you are not rigorously honest with yourself, that alone may colour your whole judgement of the candidate in his or her favour.

## Assessment plans

There are a number of different systems by which candidates can be assessed, the Seven-point Plan of Professor Alec Rodgers being one of the oldest and best known. He has identified seven headings under which candidates can be judged. They are: physical make-up; attainments; general intelligence; specific aptitudes; interests; disposition; and general circumstances. Another is John Munro Fraser's Five-fold Grading Scheme, which categorises candidates by: their impact on others; their qualifications; innate abilities; motivation; and adjustment.

The simplest and most effective system is to compare each candidate to the original person-profile you drew up (or had drawn up for you) when the vacancy was advertised. Taking each item in the profile, you can award the candidate a percentage point – education 50 per cent, personality 75 per cent, coping with stress 20 per cent and so on.

When you have gone through all the candidates in this way, you can also devise for yourself a grading system, awarding an A, B, C, D or E for each candidate. The candidate that scores an A is the most suitable; but B and C candidates are still acceptable; D candidates probably require more training and should not be accepted, whereas those who score E are unsuitable.

Some system, no matter how simple, is better than no system. Despite what some managers claim, judging a candidate by 'instincts' is unreliable and can prove costly to your company, and to you as well if your company decides you are not a good judge of character.

## Finishing unfinished business

- Make up your notes while your memory of the candidate is still fresh, getting down as many points – favourable and unfavourable – as you can. Keep them as a record of the interview.

- If you are using an assessment plan, complete it as soon as possible, otherwise you may confuse one candidate with another.

- If they did not precede the interview, set up any further tests for those candidates who are in the running, such as personality tests, technical examinations, a medical check-up, a critical review of previous work (as in the case of the creative professions such as advertising and design), presentations and so on.

- With the knowledge and consent of the candidate, take up references. References are usually sent by letter or telephone. (There is a problem with using fax, because references are always confidential, whereas fax machines, if sited in an office where anyone passing by can read them, are not, and confidentiality may be breached.)

There is increasing reluctance on the part of some employers to give more than the most superficial information about a former employee, so you may find yourself having to conduct another interview with the latter, either in a letter or on the phone, to obtain the information you need. If so, your questions should be brief and deal only with those aspects of the candidate's work that directly affect you.

- Offer the job to the successful candidate. Do not, however, reject the other possibilities until you know for certain that your first choice still wishes, and is able, to take it, otherwise you may find yourself with the vacancy still unfilled.

- 'Only hindsight,' as someone said, 'is an exact science.' If you have kept your notes of the interview together with your assessment of successful candidates, you can follow up their careers in the organisation to check how accurate your choice was. If they failed to live up to your expectations or left because they were dissatisfied with the job, you can identify where you went wrong in your interviewing and/or assessment. You can then correct your mistakes so that in future you will interview more effectively and make better choices. If, on the other hand, your choices were accurate, you can feel confident that you have developed a skill that will bring you great satisfaction and enhance your own career.

# 9

# PROBLEM-SOLVING
# INTERVIEWS

## PQRSTU

PREPARATION • QUESTIONS • RAPPORT • SKILLS • TERMINATION • UNFINISHED BUSINESS

A usually well-motivated member of staff starts to come into work later or leaves early; another can't come to terms with some new equipment; a third has been criticised and since then has been surly and unhelpful; a fourth has been drinking too much; another has a complaint about the supervisor, yet another that decisions are made without consultation.

Problems come in all shapes and sizes, and it is a test of a manager's ability how quickly and effectively they are solved. Small problems can usually be dealt with as soon as they emerge, but some take longer and need more attention. Solutions to personal problems are frequently found through talking about them to an understanding and sympathetic listener, in other words, through interviews.

Most managers, however, find it embarrassing to talk to subordinates about personal difficulties, and, feeling inadequate to the task, they prefer to sweep the problem under the carpet in the hope that it will eventually disappear. Unfortunately, it seldom does, and by the time the personal problem becomes a work problem it is often too late to take action. For this reason a number of large companies employ their own counsellors or, because people do not like to be seen talking to them, thereby revealing to their colleagues that they have a problem, outsiders.

124

For small and medium-sized companies, this can be prohibitively expensive, so it is usually left to the untrained manager on the spot to act as problem-solver. Some do it well; others not so well, and some enthusiastically seize the chance to meddle in other people's affairs, which can be a recipe for turning a minor into a major problem.

Few managers use any kind of system. They simply charge in and hope for the best. A systematic approach to the problem-solving interview can make even the most intractable problem more manageable.

# PREPARATION

You have just left your office, looking forward to your lunch, when you are approached by Kim, one of your employees, wishing to discuss something personal with you. Everything about her – posture, expression, the way she looks away when you speak to her – says that she is in some kind of trouble. You cannot postpone the lunch – it is with an important client and you made the arrangement weeks ago. What do you do?

What you *don't* do is tell Kim that you are too busy to talk and that she should come to see you later without specifying when. The unspoken message you are sending is that she is not very important and that you have more pressing matters to attend to.

What you do is explain your situation, that you can't talk, but you do not leave it like that. You go back to your office and fix an appointment to see Kim as soon as possible. Too long a delay may mean that she loses courage and the problem grows worse, because she thinks you are not really interested in hearing what she has to say. You will also need time to make some preparations of your own by checking her work record, for instance.

Most interviews are initiated by the interviewers; they define its purpose, set the time and place, and do the necessary preparation before the interview takes place. Problem-solving interviews are different. The initiator is often the interviewee who has the problem.

Managers who get around the workplace, *listening* to what their staff have to tell them, are often able to anticipate problems before they emerge, but even the most prescient miss indications that things are not what they should be and suddenly the problem is there, facing them, demanding a solution.

These are the necessary steps to take:

1. *Arrange an appointment*, convenient for both of you, when you will have time to spend with the interviewee. If it is an emergency however, you should try to deal with it then and there – or at least establish the nature of the problem at the first interview and arrange a further interview after you have had time to prepare yourself properly.

Don't squeeze problem-solving interviews between other appointments so that you have to hurry to finish. Though not open-ended, they should not be pressured. Once you have made the appointment, try not to cancel it – the employee may lose the courage or desire to speak to you. The interview should be conducted during office hours, not over a drink in the pub. This is business, not personal, and you have to remain cool and objective.

If you are initiating the interview, arrange it for an early date. The interviewee may have some idea of what you are going to talk about and any delay will make him or her more anxious and less able to discuss the problem with you.

2. *Prepare your ground.* This may not be possible to do thoroughly if the initiator is the interviewee, because you will not really know what the interview is going to be about until it starts, but you should not be caught completely off-guard. Therefore, make a practice of keeping, or having access to, up-to-date records of your team so that you can refer to them whenever necessary.

You are in a far better position to control the course of the interview if you have planned it in advance, particularly where emotions are involved. You should also keep a list of names and telephone numbers of professional advisers, doctors, lawyers, accountants and the like, whom you can recommend as and when appropriate.

It is important, however, that you do not give the names of any of your own advisers, as they may bring you into too close a contact with the person who has the problem. If your adviser and his or her adviser are one and the same, there is a danger that the work problem can slip over into your personal life, which should always be guarded against.

If the interview is in two parts, the first to find out what the problem is and the second to find the solution, you should use the period between the two to ascertain as many relevant facts as possible. This does not mean prying into matters that do not concern you; it means learning enough about the interviewee to help you make a positive contribution to the solution.

3. *Satisfy yourself on two important points*: one, do you have the authority, and two, do you have the ability, to solve the problem? If the answer is 'No' to the first, you must resist any temptation to become involved but explain the position and pass the employee on to the appropriate authority. If the answer is 'No' to the second, be honest, tell the employee, and suggest who can help. This is where the list referred to above will come in handy.

4. *Define the purpose of the interview*. Whoever initiates it, it is always your responsibility as the interviewer to establish its purpose. Until you know what the problem is, you have to spend time at the beginning determining what you want to achieve from the interview. If you are not clear in your mind, you cannot help the interviewee. Make sure the interviewee agrees to the purpose.

The purpose of problem-solving interviews is to help the interviewee understand the problem so that he or she can either resolve it in some way or, if this is not possible, come to terms with it. To do this you also have to clarify the facts so that the interviewee can see exactly what the problem is, because this in itself will help.

Remember that, for the interview to succeed, do *not*:

- try to act the psychiatrist. This is not your role and you have neither the qualifications nor the experience
- meddle in private matters that do not concern you
- use the interview as an opportunity to moralise
- give advice that you are not qualified to give

# QUESTIONS

- Until you know what the problem is, you cannot formulate problem-solving questions. Therefore, when you meet your interviewee at the interview, you can approach the subject only in the most general way, not pushing forward or trying to steer them into areas they may not wish to enter.
- Your main task at the beginning, and indeed throughout the interview, is to let the interviewee do the talking while you listen.
- Though you will have little time in which to think them out, your questions should be as carefully formulated and expressed as in other interviews.
- The kind of questions you ask should be such as to permit the interviewee to come to some understanding of the problem and then to make suggestions how it can be solved. Remember, it is for the interviewee to find the solution, not you.
- Start with general open questions to establish:

  - what the problem is
  - how the interviewee views it
  - who else may be involved in it
  - in what way if affects the interviewee

You have to prepare yourself to accept that you yourself may be part of the problem as far as the interviewee sees it, and to go on dealing with it unemotionally and objectively.

- Open questions should be followed with more specific

closed questions to ascertain all the facts as well as the interviewee's feelings about them. In problem-solving interviews facts and emotions are usually mixed up together – the events that led to the interviewee consulting you and his or her attitude to them are inextricably linked together. It is your task, as far as is possible, to separate them.

• Once you think you have got to the bottom of the problem or complaint, summarise or restate it to obtain the interviewee's consensus. 'Tell me if I've got this right. You are angry with your supervisor because . . .' You can then move on to the second stage of the interview, which is to search for a solution.

• Motivate the interviewee to talk with more open questions. Very often talking alone, getting the problem aired, is the best way to solve it. You want to get beyond the superficial to the real causes underlying it. At the same time you must avoid prying into private concerns. The line between satisfying your own genuine interest as well as your need as a manager to come to grips with the problem and invading the interviewee's privacy is thin indeed, and you cross it at your peril.

• Work on the basis of 'need to know' rather than 'want to know'. Control your natural curiosity and limit your questions strictly to what is relevant. Do not encourage interviewees to tell you things that may later embarrass or incriminate them.

# RAPPORT

Trust is a vital element in all interviews but especially in problem-solving interviews. Your aim is to earn the interviewees' trust, to get in touch with their feelings and attitudes but not to become part of them. Which means, in effect, that whatever happens during the interviews you have to retain your objectivity. This is the only way you will help them to face unpleasant truths, to change them where possible and, where not, to accept them.

You should endeavour to separate your working relationship from your role as counsellor, otherwise you will not be able to become the recipient of intimate details about the interviewees' private life. You have to indicate to them that whatever they tell you is for your ears only and for the purpose of finding a solution to the problem. However, it may happen that you have to take the matter to a higher authority, in which case you have to tell interviewees of this, otherwise they will think that you have betrayed them.

No matter how good the relationship you establish in the interview, you have to accept that you cannot change people nor can you alter their attitudes towards life. They in turn have to realise that though they may feel confident that you will support them, you are not their friend and they cannot depend on you to make things better for them.

Here are some *do's* and *don'ts* which will help to establish rapport with interviewees:

- **Do** arrange your time so that you will not have to hurry the interview. As we have seen, all interviews have their own natural pace, which the interviewer controls. The pace for problem-solving interviews has to be slower, because interviewees are often reluctant to reveal what is troubling them – even when they themselves have made the first approach.

- **Do** ensure that you will be undisturbed. Disruptions and distractions not only break the concentration, as they do in all interviews; they also destroy the atmosphere of trust and concern which may have taken you a long time to create and which you may never succeed in reviving.

- **Do** let the interviewees have the floor at the start of the interview. This will allow you to discover what it is that they want from you and, at the same time, permit them to get any anger, frustration or other strong feelings out of their system. Until this has happened, it is difficult to move beyond the emotions to their meaning, which is where solutions lie.

- **Don't** show embarrassment at what the interviewees tell

130

you, because this is another way of condemning and rejecting them. It is a test of your maturity that you listen in a calm and detached manner, your only concern being to help them solve the problem.

● **Do** remain poised and cool-headed whatever the provocation. Attempts to placate the interviewees could make things worse. If they are standing, invite them to sit down. It is harder to be angry sitting down than standing up. Remember, it is not your problem, nor is it your responsibility to solve it.

● **Don't** let your moral views interfere with morale. You may disapprove of divorce, for instance, but this is irrelevant when you are trying to help a valued, but temporarily neglectful, employee to come to terms with his or her own divorce so that he or she can return to the previous high standard of performance.

● **Don't,** on the other hand, let sympathy for the employee's situation blind your judgement.

● **Do** give constructive criticism. It is your duty as their boss to point out defects in their performance and, if necessary, to tell harsh truths about the way they are behaving, and to do so without apologising.

● **Do** listen, not only to what they tell you, but to what they leave out, because it is often in the silences and in the gaps between words that the real truth lies.

● **Do** give useful, practical suggestions; but don't tell people what to do. They either resent your giving them advice or they become dependent on it, using it to excuse their own inadequacies if things do not turn out as they hope.

● **Do** take notes, but only with the interviewee's consent and then only to record facts, not feelings. The notes may come into use at a later stage if there is any dispute about what was said. Reference to them will also help you decide what action, if any, to take.

# SKILLS

People find it much harder to talk about matters that affect them deeply than to discuss their work. They can talk about their jobs for hours, but mention a personal problem and they clam up immediately. To solve problems effectively, therefore, you need to use all the skills at your disposal, remembering that emotions lie much closer to the surface in problem-solving interviews than in other types of interview. Emotions, moreover, if allowed to get out of hand will block the way to solutions.

## Listening

This is at once the simplest and the most difficult of skills. If it were easier more people would be good at it. I worked for a man once who, because he was such an inept manager, was frequently called upon to solve problems caused by his own deficiencies. His method was to give employees a few minutes to have their say, then proceed to lecture and harangue them at great length. If he heard anything at all, it was what he wanted to hear, what fitted into his own view of the problem – and he could never understand why he could not keep his staff.

At problem-solving interviews, the more you listen, the more confident interviewees feel about talking to you and the better your chances of helping them find a solution.

It is all a matter of perception. If you look at them when they talk to you, and if they can see from the expression on your face that you are paying attention to everything they say, they will be encouraged to give full replies to your questions. If, on the other hand, you look away, or if they see boredom, lack of interest or disapproval in your expression, they will withdraw into themselves.

Good listening is more than just registering words like a tape recorder. It means:

- being patient and letting interviewees talk without interruption

- hearing the feelings (of hurt, anger, frustration) that lie behind the words
- studying their body language for revealing expressions and gestures
- hearing what they actually say, not what your bias or prejudice wants you to hear
- being tolerant and unshockable even if you have strong moral objections to their (private) behaviour.

## Probing

People do not always say what they mean or mean what they say. Someone coming to you with complaints about the heating in the office, trouble with another member of the staff or lack of opportunities for advancement may be telling the truth, but the complaints may also hide other, more personal and less tractable problems.

Your job is to probe – gently, tactfully but persistently – to find out what lies behind the grumbles, as far as it is within your authority, so that you can get to the root cause of them and resolve them.

Probing means:

- not accepting every fact or statement at face value
- not letting potentially significant remarks and asides pass without examining them
- not being satisfied with clichés and bland answers
- getting to the truths behind the half-truths
- recognising the evasions
- detecting the lies

It also means:

- repeating the same question but in a slightly different way
- remaining silent to encourage the interviewee to give fuller replies

- pretending ignorance or uncertainty and calling on the interviewee to supply the information
- summarising the last points made by the interviewee
- reflecting, that is repeating the interviewee's last reply but in a slightly different way, as in the following exchange:

Interviewee: 'I'm getting nowhere in this company.'
Interviewer: 'Do you mean that nobody recognises your abilities?'

- using encouraging verbalisms such as 'Uh-huh', 'Mm-mmm', 'I see', 'I understand' and so on
- guiding the interviewee away from irrelevances to the central issues, that is, not merely the events or circumstances that are causing the problems, but his or her attitudes towards them.

# TERMINATION

'In my beginning is my end,' the poet T. S. Eliot wrote, and the same thought could apply to all forms of interviewing. The beginning of the interview – defining its purpose – should coincide with its end – the accomplishment of that purpose. In all effective interviewing there should be an interrelationship between each step, so that where one ends the next starts and the division between them is virtually undetectable.

For problem-solving interviews, the purpose is not to solve the problem as such – it may not be in your power to do so – but to help the interviewee understand what the problem is and to see a way to solving it.

How long should a problem-solving interview last?

As with all types of interviews, it should not be open-ended. You and your interviewee's time are valuable, you are both on a team that has its own goals to fulfil, and giving too much of your day to one member or one subject can throw the team out of kilter. Also, by concentrating on one subject, it takes on more weight than it need do. Longer than an hour and there is a danger of the interview turning into a conversation, which means that you will no longer be fully in control and the purpose will not be achieved.

If the problem is deep-seated you may have to set up more than one meeting. Give interviewees the feeling that you are available to them when they need you, but not that you are at their disposal, otherwise they may become dependent on you, which is only going to create more problems for both of you.

You have been supportive, you have created the right atmosphere, you have given the interviewee a fair hearing, now what do you do?

Five steps to terminate the interview:

- *Indicate firmly when the end is approaching* by asking if interviewees would like to add anything more to what has been discussed and summarising what has been decided so far.

- *Thank the interviewee for talking to you* (and mean it!), even if it was the interviewee who initiated the interview. No matter how pressed you are for time, do not leave interviewees with the feeling that they are being rejected.

- *Agree with the interviewee on a plan of action.* Interviewees should not be left 'in the air', as it were, but should have specific tasks to carry out which they themselves, through your gentle probing, have suggested. Remember, though, it is their problem, not yours, so you should not undertake to do anything which will relieve them of responsibility.

- *Discourage further interviews* until the interviewee has carried out what you agreed on. If you are an empathetic and interested interviewer, the interviewee will enjoy being interviewed by you and consequently it can become a substitute for action.

- *Set up another meeting if necessary,* but not too far in the future – no more than a few days. The sooner the problem is dealt with the better. Delaying may make it worse.

# UNFINISHED BUSINESS

People's problems damage the overall effectiveness of a team or an organisation, and your ability to solve them is the measure by which you are judged as a manager. Fortunately most of them are small and can be dealt with quickly, but some require more time.

*Though not all managers realise this, the interview is still the most effective method by which the majority of problems can be solved.*

Interviewing, as we have seen, is a continuing process and an integral part of managing, which means that after the interview you continue to maintain contact with the interviewee and do not give up your interest until you are satisfied that the problem is solved.

After the interview:

- Write up your notes as soon as possible so that you can still remember how the interviewee answered, as this may be just as important as what the interviewee said. A record should be kept, particularly if the interview involved a complaint, as it may be necessary to refer back to it at a later stage.

- Even if the immediate problem has been solved, follow up any suggestions or plans agreed at the interview. This is important, not only to ascertain that appropriate action has been taken, but also to assure the interviewee of your continuing interest and concern.

- Whoever initiated the interview in the first instance, make a further appointment with the interviewee to check on progress. Don't wait too long, as problems have a bad habit of appearing to solve themselves whereas in fact they have only gone underground and, just when you think they have gone away, re-assert themselves, usually at the most awkward times.

# 10

# DISCIPLINARY AND EXIT INTERVIEWS

## PQRSTU

PREPARATION • QUESTIONS • RAPPORT • SKILLS • TERMINATION • UNFINISHED BUSINESS

This chapter covers disciplinary, resignation and dismissal interviews. The last two are generally known as 'exit' interviews.

The reason I have put them together is that, regrettably, despite counselling, some employees continue to perform disappointingly or downright badly. This leads to reprimands, and sometimes, if thought appropriate, further training; but in the end, if no appreciable improvement is shown or if the employees are clearly unsuited to the job, the manager has no alternative but to dismiss them. In some cases, they decide to go on their own accord and they resign. (There are other reasons, of course, for an employee resigning, as we shall see below.)

Another reason for putting the three types of interview together is that they have a number of points in common:

• Change is the key to all of them. The purpose of disciplinary interviews is, in the main, to change the performance and behaviour of the interviewee; but they may also involve changing the manager's approach to the people he or she works with. The departure from an organisation of an employee will obviously result in a major change to the employee's circumstances, and to a lesser extent to the manager who has had to deal with the problem and to the organisation itself.

● All have the potential to be emotional, anxiety-producing interviews – for both participants. Obviously, employees do not like to be disciplined, nor do they like to lose their jobs, so for them these interviews will produce a wide range of reactions from hurt and disbelief to anger and resentment. The managers, too, may suffer painful emotions, especially if they have been directly involved in the circumstances leading to the dismissal; and all but the coldest and most aloof manager (certainly not the ideal) will find the experience nerve-racking.

● They are easy to handle badly, not only for the reason given above, but also because the temptations to resort to personal attack, to repeat old arguments and to exchange blame and recriminations are sometimes difficult to resist.

● They all have to be dealt with coolly and systematically. They are at the end of a continuum beginning with the problem behaviour, and by the time the interview takes place, they may have built up a considerable 'head of steam'.

Some managers doubt whether there is any point in conducting exit interviews. They believe that you discipline by telling the employee what to do, you dismiss by telling the employee to go, and if the employee wants to go why waste time talking about it?

Managers who think that way are not, I hope, beyond persuading that these interviews are essential for the following reasons:

● From employees who are resigning, management can learn about weaknesses in the company, in other employees and in management itself, because leavers are freer to talk about their jobs than those still in employment. Truths may be told that would not otherwise be revealed.

● If the employee is leaving for a higher salary, the company can find out what the competition is paying or what extra benefits are being offered.

● Employers can also learn that they are employing too many people who are dissatisfied with, and unchallenged by, the low standards expected from them, thus improving selection processes in the future and reducing staff turnover.

● They are an excellent opportunity for good public relations. Companies can show that they are good employers who treat their people fairly by listening to their side of the story, and, more important, by awarding them generous severance payments.

# PREPARATION

1. **Define your purpose.** For the disciplinary interview, this is in order to

● improve performance and, where possible, prevent further breaches of company policy
● let the employees come to terms with what has gone wrong so that they can correct their behaviour

For resignation and dismissal interviews, your purpose is to

● get feedback from former employees about any hidden management problems
● learn about selection procedures in order to improve them
● give the employee a fair hearing, and
● improve the image of the company

2. **Plan the interview.**
● Satisfy yourself that you have given the employee every opportunity to change his or her behaviour or improve his or her performance, and that you have removed any obstacles to their achievement.
● Make sure that, in dismissing the employee, you are

acting within the law. Dismissals are fraught with legal pit-falls, which makes some managers think they can never fire anyone. In fact you can dismiss unsatisfactory employees, but you first must ensure that you are not contravening employment protection legislation.

• Learn as much as you can about the individual that is relevant to the forthcoming interview. This entails consulting the work records and personnel file, and finding out from his or her supervisor and others about the employee's recent behaviour and performance. It may also mean finding out about family background, *but only as it affects the outcome of the interview*.

• Gather as much hard evidence as you can about the circumstances leading to the disciplinary or exit interview. The employee is more likely to accept the facts if you have them at your fingertips than if you are merely levelling vague accusations.

• Be sure to bring with you to the interview all relevant records and files for easy reference.

• From what you know about the individual and the circumstances, plan how you intend to pace the interview and what questions you will ask. Write them down if necessary, but do not attempt to learn them off by heart.

• Do not conduct the interview on the spur of the moment, when you may still be full of anger. Arrange it in advance, when you will have had time to calm down. It is part of the false machismo in some managements to dismiss subordinates in an apparent fit of rage, enjoying the sense of power it gives them. They also hope that the employees will tell others, so that the management's reputation for toughness will get around in that particular industry. This is an altogether wrongheaded and absurd view of what management is all about and in the end it does the organisation no good at all, because good people will not want to work for it.

• There is never a good day or a good time of day to fire someone, but if possible avoid just before the weekend or a holiday. Dismissing employees late on a Friday means they have all weekend with little else to do but brood which, if you want the interview to have ultimately a positive outcome, is neither wise nor fair.

● Choose an office where you can be sure of privacy. This is definitely not the time to have to contend with constant interruptions and distractions. Some writers recommend that you use an office which is neutral to both of you, as this will reduce the inequalities and make for a more positive and mutually acceptable outcome.

● Resolve to go into the interview with an open mind and not to prejudge any of the issues.

# QUESTIONS

If you have prepared properly for the interview, you will have established as much as possible of the background leading to the discipline, dismissal or resignation, and will have brought with you all the relevant records so that you can refer to them if necessary.

Your next step is to ask questions which will obtain (1) the interviewee's confirmation of the facts, and (2) his or her reasons for what has happened.

Questions perform another valuable function at these interviews: they take the sting out of the hurt and anger. As long as you are calmly asking them and the interviewee is answering them, neither of you can get into pointless rows and recriminations.

If the purpose of the interview is to *discipline* employees, you have to find out whether or not they know

● what the job required
● what stopped it from being performed properly
● what they are willing to do in the future to ensure that the job is properly performed, and, most important,
● what options are left to you if they do not do so

This last question leaves the interviewees to state the consequences of lack of proper performance, namely dismissal. Eliciting this from them in this way is far more effective than threatening that, if they don't do better in the future, you will have to fire them.

If the *dismissal* results from doing something that was against the policy of the company, your questions will be directed towards establishing two vital issues:

- whether or not the interviewee knew what that policy was, and if not, why not
- that the interviewee knew that the actions complained of were in breach of that policy

In the case of *resignation* interviews, where employees are leaving for their own reasons (as when they have been offered another job at a better salary or are moving to another part of the country), you can find out from them a lot more about the way your organisation works than you can from someone currently employed there. The interviewees will not have any bitterness towards it, and in fact may feel well disposed towards it, but at the same time will have the benefit of hindsight as well as a more objective viewpoint on which you can base future management decisions.

You will want to find out what the circumstances were that led to the resignation; and, if it has come without warning, you will also want to know what prevented the leaver from speaking to you sooner.

In more general terms, you will also want to know

- what, in the interviewee's view, creates a productive working atmosphere
- to what extent these features were present in the interviewee's own circumstances
- to what extent they were missing and why
- how far the leaver was supported by management (this may include you, so be prepared!)

- what changes could be made to improve working conditions
- if the leaver is going to another job, what benefits were offered in case you can match them, in the future if not now

For disciplinary and exit interviews, your questions should strive for mutual understanding, not confrontation. Remember, this is an interview, not an interrogation.

In particular, you should ask:

- *Open questions* which will allow the erring employee to accept the facts and, in a disciplinary interview, agree to change his or her behaviour. For example: 'Why do you think this happened?', 'What do you think led to this?', 'What are your feelings about this?', 'What are you going to do to change?' This way you do not impose your view on the events, nor do you tell employees what has to be done, but you leave it to them to come to decisions about their past and future behaviour.
- *Clear and unambiguous questions.* If the interviewee is taking the interview lightly, or being aggressive or facetious, you may have to repeat your questions, perhaps in a slightly different form, to indicate how seriously you treat the matter. For example:

'What happened between you that led to the fight in the canteen?'

'The place just isn't big enough for the two of us.'

'Could you please tell me how the fight started?'

'What difference does it make? It's over with, isn't it?'

'You wouldn't be here if it was. The fight may be over but the consequences aren't. So how did it begin?'

Do not ask:

- *Leading questions* that force interviewees to answer as you want them to. For instance, if you had asked, 'What made you start that fight in the canteen?' you would be making the assumption, perhaps incorrect, that the interviewee was the responsible party.

• *Questions that trap the interviewee.* 'Would you describe yourself as honest?' Interviewees are unlikely to answer negatively, which means they are tricked into defending themselves even before they know what the specific accusation is. Trick questions also include those that indicate by the way they are worded how you want the interviewee to reply: 'Is this the sort of thing an honest person does?'

• *Vague questions:* 'Been in some trouble lately, I hear?'

• *Self-incriminating questions* that force the interviewee to admit guilt: 'Everyone I've spoken to says you started the fight. Are you calling them all liars?'

# RAPPORT

Disciplinary interviews, despite their apparent negative elements, are in fact positive in outcome, because, as we have seen, their purpose is to produce change in the behaviour or performance of employees. When they do not succeed and employees have to be dismissed or they decide to leave, the exit interview can still be useful in that it can help to encourage continued change and growth in employees after they are no longer in your employ.

Even if you dismiss this as an idealistic goal, exit interviews should still be conducted, if only to allow employees a final opportunity to give their side of the story.

Here are some helpful hints on how to establish and maintain rapport even in the most difficult and awkward interviews, where emotions are so close to the surface they are likely to burst out at any moment.

## Maintaining rapport in difficult interviews

• Approach the interview with inner strength and control, not by bullying the interviewee or abusing your power but by the way you hold yourself, the way you speak to the interviewee and the professional way you conduct the proceedings.

- If you dislike the interviewee, admitting it to yourself will free you of embarrassment and you can deal with the matter calmly and objectively.

- If you have to criticise, do so without feeling the need to defend yourself or to apologise for doing what is, after all, your job.

- Remember always to treat interviewees as you would wish to be treated if you were in their shoes.

- Prepare the room to ensure privacy and quiet. Try, if possible, to sit near the interviewee – not more than a metre or two away. If you remain behind your desk it makes the interview more of a confrontation.

- Greet interviewees in a friendly way; let them settle down, then start straight in without any preliminaries. They probably know the reason for the interview, and the longer you delay getting to the point, the more apprehensive and defensive they will become.

- Set out the facts as you know them and explain why they are being dismissed. Do not drag out the reasons.

- Make it clear that the decision is irreversible, otherwise you will find yourself involved either in fending off pleas for reconsideration, which will be embarrassing for both of you, or in defending your decision.

- Invite the interviewees to give their side of the story, explaining that you are looking for explanations, not excuses. Again, do not let this drag out. The quicker the better for both of you.

- Do not attack them personally, rather describe the circumstances leading to the dismissal.

- Do not allow the interviewee to manipulate you through sympathy, but remain calm, composed and in control.

- Always give dismissed employees a chance to let off steam, but do not

    – argue with them
    – lose your temper

- encourage them to criticise or tell tales on others
- patronise them or treat them like naughty children
- defend company policy

## Coping with strong emotions

When told they are being dismissed, employees react in different ways depending on the kind of people they are. For ease of reference, I have divided them up into five possible types and have suggested how to handle them. It is important to point out, however, that they are only *types* and you cannot predict exactly how people will behave, no matter how well you know them, until they are actually faced with the dismissal.

The five categories are:

Attackers
Defenders
Lawyers
Philosophers
Weepers

**Attackers** feel rage and hurt. They react by shouting at you or the company, or by showing contempt and disgust for the way they have been treated. Some are more open about their anger than others. It is best to get the anger out into the open so that you can get on with the other, more important matters. Remain calm and objective. Don't trade insults or go on the defensive. Keep to the facts and offer any helpful advice.

**Defenders** accept with reluctance that they have done wrong, but they are so consumed with fear for their future that they will plead with you to reconsider your decision. Explain that the fault lies with both of you: you were wrong to employ them and they were wrong to take the job, but do not enter into any discussions about, or agree to a postpone-ment of, your decision. Show them that you are concerned for their future and give them details of agencies that may help them.

**Lawyers** are as angry and hurt as the attackers but they do not show it. Instead, they convert it into revenge. They want you to suffer as they have, and because they have some knowledge of employment legislation, they threaten to use it against you. Before you reach the dismissal interview, you should know as much about your rights – and theirs – as they do. Do not treat their threats lightly, nor let them frighten you into taking rash decisions. Let them state their case and respond in a firm and formal manner. You cannot, of course, stop them from taking action against you if they think they have a case for wrongful dismissal, but point out that legal representation can cost money and they may lose.

**Philosophers** may have anticipated your actions and have prepared themselves for it. They may even be relieved that one of you has taken the inevitable decision. To the employer, their shoulder-shrugging indifference to the news is sometimes more disconcerting than anger or tears. However, their apparent stoicism could also be hiding shock and disbelief. Invite specific questions from them and suggest they consult a career counsellor if they are uncertain what to do next.

**Weepers** are probably dreaded (especially by male managers) more than any of the others, because their employers are made to feel helpless and guilty. Embarrassed, they respond either with irritation – 'Why are you making such a fuss. It's only a job!' – or with an excess of sympathy – 'I know how awful this must be for you, but I'm sure it's the best thing in the long run.' (Women, in the main, handle weepers more professionally; they are able to balance genuine concern with doing their job.) Weepers are likely to feel just as embarrassed as interviewers, who need to show a little patience and tact to allow them to recover their composure. Accept the fact that you cannot make things right for them. All you can offer is a tissue if they need one, a modicum of reassurance and, more practically, the names of some useful agencies which they can contact if they need further assistance.

In contrast to disciplinary and dismissal interviews, in resignation interviews you may have interviewees who are eager to move on to other, better, jobs. You have to accept this with good grace and show interest in their future. Surliness and indignation in the face of their happiness is a sign of immaturity and reveals a low state of morale in your team. Be pleased for them, knowing that the experience they got from working for you reflects well on your organisation.

# SKILLS

In disciplinary interviews, you should do your job, however unpleasant it may be, in a calm, controlled, professional way, maintaining your poise and equilibrium in the face of the interviewee's reactions. Your greatest skill lies in your inner strength, not in showing the interviewee how tough you are or how much power you wield, and in so doing you will minimise the interviewee's reactions and make the interview a positive process from which you both can learn.

In particular, you should:

● Use summaries to calm down interviewees and to reassure them that you are taking the matter seriously. Summaries also give them the opportunity to correct any errors of fact. ('Let me see if I've got this right. You say that the reason you're not keeping up with your sales figures is that production isn't putting through your orders quickly enough?')

● Direct interviewees away from irrelevances. They may blame others, including yourself, for what has happened to them, or claim that the organisation itself is at fault. ('I don't want to get into arguments about this with you – it's not very useful. Let's just say we agree to differ and go on to other matters of more immediate importance.')

● In resignation interviews, probe to find why the leaver is resigning. Is it poor training or bad equipment, for instance? Find out how the leaver thinks things can be improved.

('You've hinted that the team you were part of is not working well together. Could you be more specific?') Use restatements to make sure that the facts given to you are correct. If you fail to do this, your company may get a wrong impression of why this particular employee is resigning and this could reduce the interview's effectiveness.

● Be willing to listen, not just to the words spoken, but to the unspoken ones that hide the hurt, anger and pain. Within the time limit, let employees talk freely until they can accept with a certain degree of calm your reasons for the termination.

● Pay attention to tone of voice, observe posture and mannerisms for clues to the interviewee's feelings, and adjust your own contribution to the interview accordingly. Remember, even though this may be the last time you interview the leaver, he or she is still entitled to your full attention.

# TERMINATION

Some practical hints:

● Keep disciplinary and exit interviews short. They should not be allowed to drag on longer than fifteen to twenty minutes. Five minutes ought to be sufficient to go over the details of the offence or the reasons for the resignation, five minutes to hear the interviewee's side of the story, and the remainder to deal with the financial arrangements.

● Make appointments for further interviews, if necessary. In a disciplinary interview, you will probably want to assess how seriously your criticisms and the employee's undertakings to change his or her behaviour have been put into effect. You will need a follow-up interview.

● In a resignation interview, if you are trying to persuade the employee to stay in your employment, you may need two or three interviews to break a deadlock. You should not leave the employee in a state of uncertainty but set out a clear agenda of what you intend to do in the immediate future so that the employee knows that the matter is being taken seriously. If, despite your efforts, the employee resigns, your company will have done its best and its reputation as a fair employer will remain intact – something which will reassure the rest of the staff.

• If the problem leading to the interview has arisen from the initial unsuitability of the employee for the job, it does no harm to acknowledge the fact. It may lead to better selection procedures in the future as well as better interviewing practices.

• Think of the disciplinary and exit interviews as a combination of 'good news' and 'bad news'. Your job as a skilful manager is to bring an unsatisfactory situation to a satisfactory conclusion, not to destroy people's self-esteem. You do not want employees to leave with bitterness, if you can avoid it. Obviously, you cannot be responsible for what happens to them in the future, but they should leave your office believing that they have a future.

• Do not lean over backwards to be pleasant to them. They should know how you feel. But, by referring to the requirements of the job rather than their personal failings, you take the edge off the criticism or dismissal.

• Resist the temptation to make terminated employees offers that you cannot carry out just to get them out of your office. Carefully go through the severance arrangements with them, describing payments and benefits, and make it clear that you are not going to negotiate any other deals with them.

• Do not offer advice unless requested and you know what you are talking about. Nothing is more galling to someone who has just been fired than to hear a manager telling them what he or she thinks they should do next.

• Do not suggest looking into any other arrangements on their behalf after the interview is over. As soon as they leave your office, the termination is complete.

• Have names and addresses or agencies and organisations such as a career counsellor at hand in case you are asked for specific help, but otherwise do not offer the employee any further assistance.

- As you would with any other interviewee, thank them for their time. Offer them good wishes for their future. Whatever their offence, they are still entitled to be treated with dignity, and you have to keep in mind your own and your company's reputation as decent, fair-minded employers.

## UNFINISHED BUSINESS

- Always write up your notes as soon as possible after the interview is over and keep them in a safe place where you can refer to them later should the interview lead to any legal proceedings (for wrongful dismissal, for example).
- Evaluate the information or suggestions you received from the interviewees in the course of the interview about the way the organisation is run, and check the truth of any complaints against individuals. You may find that what you have been told corresponds with your own observation or the observation of others who have recently left the company. If a certain trend has been identified, it must be investigated before it becomes a serious problem.
- If low morale has been identified as one of the trends, check the attitudes of colleagues working in the same team as to their own state of morale.
- The interviewee's unsuitability for the job may have resulted either from a wrong job specification or poor recruitment interviewing. If necessary, revise the job specification, and if you think that interviewing techniques are at fault, arrange for those responsible to have further training. (They should, of course, also be encouraged to buy this book.)

# INDEX